Student Activity Guide for

Learning for Earning

by

John A. Wanat
Author of Vocational Education Materials
and
National Consultant on Cooperative Education
Freehold, New Jersey

E. Weston Pfeiffer
Education Program Specialist
New Jersey State Department of Education
Division of Vocational Education
Trenton, New Jersey

Richard Van Gulik
Principal, Salem County Vocational Technical School
Woodstown, New Jersey

South Holland, Illinois
THE GOODHEART-WILLCOX COMPANY, INC.
Publishers

INTRODUCTION

This Student Activity Guide is designed for use with the text, *Learning for Earning: Your Route to Success*. It will help you understand and remember the facts and concepts presented in the text about cooperative education and career exploration. It will also help you apply this learning to your everyday life.

The activities in this guide are divided into chapters that correspond to the chapters in the text. By reading the text first, you will have the information you need to complete the activities. Try to complete the activities without referring to the text. If necessary, you can look at the book again later to complete any questions you could not answer. At that time, you can also compare the answers you have to the information in the book.

You will find a number of types of activities in this guide. Each chapter starts with a crossword puzzle, word maze, matching, or fill-in-the-blank activity to help reinforce your vocabulary. These activities allow you to practice using new terms introduced in the text. Activities like these have "right" answers. They can be used as review guides when you study for test and quizzes. Some of the other activities, such as evaluations and comparisons, will ask for opinions and ideas that cannot be judged as "right" or "wrong." These activities are designed to stimulate your thinking and help you apply information presented in the text.

The activities in this guide have been designed to increase your interest and understanding of the text material. The more thought you put into the activities, the more knowledge you will gain from them.

Copyright 1991

by

THE GOODHEART-WILLCOX COMPANY, INC.

All rights reserved. No part of this book may be reproduced, stored in a retrieval system, or transmitted in any form or by any means, electronic, mechanical, photocopying, recording, or otherwise, without the prior written permission of The Goodheart-Willcox Company, Inc. Manufactured in the United States of America.

International Standard Book Number 0-87006-795-8

234567890-91-9876543

CONTENTS

	Activity Guide	Text

part one
YOU, SCHOOL, AND WORK

1 **The Importance of Work** 7 11
    A. Reinforcing Vocabulary
    B. Your Thoughts on Work
    C. Working to Help Others
    D. Careers That Meet Your Goals

2 **Education and Training** 11 19
    A. Reinforcing Vocabulary
    B. Basic Skills for the Workplace
    C. Past, Present, and Future Jobs
    D. Plans for Career Training

3 **Time Management and Study Skills** 15 29
    A. Reinforcing Vocabulary
    B. Time Log
    C. Time Log Review
    D. IRS Time
    E. Good and Poor Study Habits

4 **Cooperative Education** 21 39
    A. Reiniforcing Vocabulary
    B. Co-op Interview
    C. A Self-Evaluation
    D. Understanding Cooperative Education

5 **Vocational Student Organizations** 25 50
    A. Reinforcing Vocabulary
    B. Learning About Vocational Organizations
    C. Your Vocational Organization
    D. Being a Good Leader

part two
MATCHING YOURSELF WITH A CAREER

6 **Your Resources, Values, and Goals** 29 62
    A. Reinforcing Vocabulary
    B. Career Interests and Abilities Inventory
    C. Your Personality Traits
    D. Setting and Reaching Goals

	Activity Guide	Text

7 Decisions 35 73
    A. Reinforcing Vocabulary
    B. The Decision-Making Process
    C. Trade-offs
    D. Preparing for Career Decisions
    E. Making Decisions at Work

8 Types of Careers 41 82
    A. Reinforcing Vocabulary
    B. Occupational Research
    C. Exploring Career Clusters

part three
FINDING AND KEEPING A JOB

9 The Job Search 47 104
    A. Reinforcing Vocabulary
    B. Want Ad Abbreviations
    C. Using Want Ads
    D. Resume Worksheet
    E. Applying for Employment

10 Interviews 53 113
    A. Reinforcing Vocabulary
    B. Company Research
    C. Interview Questions
    D. Follow Up in Writing
    E. Interview Practices

11 Winning at Work 59 126
    A. Reinforcing Vocabulary
    B. If You Were an Employer
    C. Winners or Losers?
    D. Winning Work Habits

12 Being a Team Player 63 137
    A. Reinforcing Vocabulary
    B. Tips for Getting Along
    C. Studying Work Attitudes
    D. Good Work Habits in Action

13 Changes in Job Status 69 149
    A. Reinforcing Vocabulary
    B. Starting Full-time Work
    C. Changing Jobs
    D. Leaving a Job
    E. Job Changes Through a Career
    F. Report on Changes

	Activity Guide	Text

part four
PERSONAL DEVELOPMENT AND JOB SUCCESS

14 Basic Skills 75 162
    A. Reinforcing Vocabulary
    B. Strengthening Your Vocabulary
    C. Proofreading for Accuracy
    D. Math Practice

15 Communication 79 171
    A. Reinforcing Vocabulary
    B. Speech Evaluation
    C. Telephone Practice
    D. Writing Business Letters
    E. Understanding Body Language

16 Appearance and Clothing 85 186
    A. Reinforcing Vocabulary
    B. Check Your Grooming Habits
    C. What Workers Wear
    D. Wardrobe Planning for Work

17 Health 89 196
    A. Reinforcing Vocabulary
    B. A Balanced Diet
    C. Learning About Stress
    D. Avoiding Substance Abuse at Work

18 Safety on the Job 93 209
    A. Reinforcing Vocabulary
    B. Preventing Accidents
    C. Understanding Safety Practices

part five
MONEY MANAGEMENT

19 Paychecks and Taxes 97 230
    A. Reinforcing Vocabulary
    B. Completing a Tax Return
    C. Reading a Paycheck Stub

20 Budgets 101 245
    A. Reinforcing Vocabulary
    B. Fixed and Flexible Expenses
    C. Making Your Money Work for You
    D. Planning a Budget

21 Checking Accounts 105 254
    A. Reinforcing Vocabulary
    B. Using a Checking Account
    C. Balancing a Checkbook
    D. Correcting an Imbalance

	Activity Guide	Text

22 Savings 111 267
   A. Reinforcing Vocabulary
   B. Savings Survey
   C. Financial Institutions
   D. Savings Deposits and Withdrawals

23 Credit 115 277
   A. Reinforcing Vocabulary
   B. Credit Advantages and Disadvantages
   C. The Cost of Credit
   D. The Credit Game

24 Insurance 119 289
   A. Reinforcing Vocabulary
   B. Understanding Insurance
   C. Car Insurance Costs
   D. Personal Property Inventory

part six
BEING INDEPENDENT

25 A Place to Live 123 302
   A. Reinforcing Vocabulary
   B. Apartment Search
   C. Furnishing an Apartment
   D. Housing Costs

26 Transportation 127 312
   A. Reinforcing Vocabulary
   B. Reading a Bus Schedule
   C. Transportation Comparison

27 Being a Responsible Citizen 131 321
   A. Reinforcing Vocabulary
   B. Citizen Awareness
   C. Voters' Survey
   D. Classroom Council
   E. Legal Advice
   F. Writing a Complaint Letter

28 Entrepreneurship 137 334
   A. Reinforcing Vocabulary
   B. Retail and Business Services
   C. Is Entrepreneurship for You?
   D. Business Advice
   E. Planning a Business
   F. Business Organizations

# 1 THE IMPORTANCE OF WORK

REINFORCING VOCABULARY

Activity A Name _____

Chapter 1 Date _____ Period _____

Read each of the definitions below and decide which chapter term is being defined. Write the correct terms in the blanks and transfer your answers to the crossword puzzle.

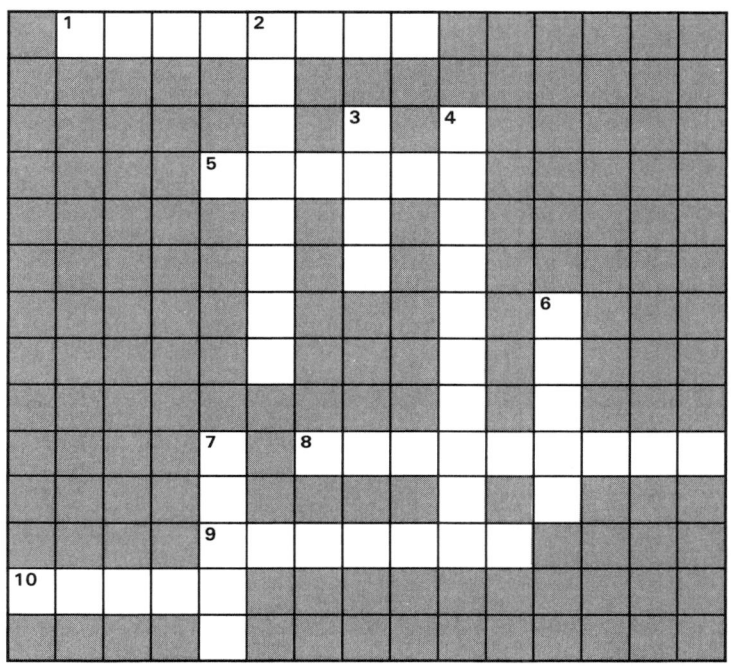

Across

_____ 1. Work hours that are not firmly set and may change on a daily or weekly basis.

_____ 5. The amount of money a person receives for doing a job.

_____ 8. Typical way of life.

_____ 9. A country's way of producing, distributing, and consuming goods and services.

_____ 10. Work hours that are firmly set and do not change.

Down

_____ 2. The sum of traits that distinguish a person as an individual.

_____ 3. An activity done to produce or accomplish something.

_____ 4. A person's confidence in himself or herself.

_____ 6. Items a person would like to have, but does not require.

_____ 7. The basics a person must have in order to live.

YOUR THOUGHTS ON WORK

Activity B   Name _____

Chapter 1   Date _____ Period _____

Begin thinking about how your work will fit into your life. Do so by filling in answers to the following questions. Then discuss your ideas in class.

1. You will probably have a job because you need income to live. List three other important reasons why you will work.

    a. _____

    b. _____

    c. _____

2. List three benefits you hope to gain from working.

    a. _____

    b. _____

    c. _____

3. List five qualities you think are important to job success in any type of job.

    a. _____

    b. _____

    c. _____

    d. _____

    e. _____

4. What type of work interests you and why? _____
_____
_____
_____

5. What special qualities would help you succeed in the type of work that interests you? _____
_____
_____
_____

6. How would doing this type of work affect your lifestyle? _____
_____
_____
_____

WORKING TO HELP OTHERS

Activity C   Name _____

Chapter 1   Date _____ Period _____

Throughout history, many people have chosen to do work that helps others. These people are often successful without making a lot of money. Success comes to them in the form of pride and satisfaction in helping others. Answer the following questions about people who work to help society.

1. Name three famous people, living or dead, who have contributed to others while living a simple lifestyle. Include a short statement of each person's accomplishments.

    a. _____

    b. _____

    c. _____

2. Name three people you know who have contributed to others while living a simple lifestyle. Write a short statement of what each person has done.

    a. _____

    b. _____

    c. _____

3. If you were given the chance to talk to any interesting person who works to help others, who would you choose and why?

    _____

4. List three qualities that most people who work to help others have in common.

    _____

5. What would you like to contribute to society during your own life?

    _____

CAREERS THAT MEET YOUR GOALS

Activity D　　　　　　　　　Name _____

Chapter 1　　　　　　　　　Date _____ Period _____

Whether or not you reach many of your goals in life will depend on the career you choose. List some of your goals related to each topic in the chart. Then list careers that you think would help you meet your goals.

	Your Goals	Careers to Help You Meet Your Goals
1. Income		
2. Identity		
3. Lifestyle		
4. Satisfaction		

2 EDUCATION AND TRAINING

REINFORCING VOCABULARY

Activity A
Chapter 2

Name _____

Date _____ Period _____

Match the following terms with their correct definitions.

_____ 1. Refers to the use of automated equipment to do mechanical tasks.

_____ 2. System that allows a person to type information into a computer where it is stored until it is needed.

_____ 3. Skills, such as reading, writing, and math, that are required for any career.

_____ 4. Training that involves learning a trade by working under the direction and guidance of a skilled worker.

_____ 5. Degree usually received after completing two years of education beyond high school.

_____ 6. Programs in the areas of health, business, agriculture, skilled trades, and marketing that may be offered to students who are still in high school.

_____ 7. Degree usually received after completing a four-year-program beyond high school.

_____ 8. An arrangement between schools and places of employment that allows students to receive on-the-job training.

_____ 9. When people work at home on computers and send their work to the office through the computer.

_____ 10. Change that makes machines more productive by getting rid of older machines or operations done by hand.

_____ 11. Courses that prepare people for the impact computers are having on society.

a. Apprenticeship.
b. Associate degree.
c. Bachelor degree.
d. Basic skills.
e. Computer literacy courses.
f. Cooperative education.
g. Robotics.
h. Technological change.
i. Telecommuting.
j. Vocational training.
k. Word processing.

BASIC SKILLS FOR THE WORKPLACE

Activity B   Name _____

Chapter 2   Date _____ Period _____

Basic reading, writing, and math skills are necessary in all jobs. To be a successful worker, you will need these skills as well as occupational skills. Complete the charts below by identifying two occupations that interest you. List the tasks that you think people do in those occupations and the basic skills needed for those tasks. Then decide whether you have the skills needed to perform those tasks.

Occupation 1: _____

Tasks	Basic Skills Needed
1.	
2.	
3.	

Do you have the skills needed to perform the tasks listed above? If not, what can you do now to develop the skills?
_____
_____
_____

Occupation 2: _____

Tasks	Basic Skills Needed
1.	
2.	
3.	

Do you have the skills needed to perform the tasks listed above? If not, what can you do now to develop the skills?
_____
_____
_____

PAST, PRESENT, AND FUTURE JOBS

Activity C   Name _____

Chapter 2   Date _____ Period _____

In today's world, technology changes rapidly. New jobs are created to replace jobs that exist. Workers use new and different skills. Consider these advances in technology as you complete this activity. Then discuss your ideas in class.

1. Make a list of jobs from the past that no longer exist due to changes in technology. Describe what new jobs have taken their place. _____
   _____
   _____
   _____
   _____
   _____

2. List some current jobs that you think may also be phased out due to advances in technology. _____
   _____
   _____
   _____
   _____
   _____

3. Describe some new jobs you think might be created in the future due to advances in technology.
   _____
   _____
   _____
   _____

4. What jobs of the future appeal to you? _____
   _____
   _____
   _____
   _____

5. What can you do to prepare for the jobs of the future? _____
   _____
   _____
   _____
   _____
   _____

PLANS FOR CAREER TRAINING

Activity D   Name _____

Chapter 2   Date _____ Period _____

Many different forms of career training are available. The training that is best for you depends upon your own career goals. For each type of training, describe a career goal a person who is enrolled in the program could have. Describe advantages of using that form of training to help meet the career goal described.

Vocational programs: _____

_____

_____

Cooperative education: _____

_____

_____

Apprenticeships: _____

_____

_____

Colleges and universities: _____

_____

_____

Company training programs: _____

_____

_____

Military training: _____

_____

_____

Describe three careers that you might like to train for in the future. Describe the form of training you would use for each career. Give your reasons for choosing that form of training.

a. _____

_____

_____

_____

b. _____

_____

_____

_____

c. _____

_____

_____

_____

3 TIME MANAGEMENT AND STUDY SKILLS

REINFORCING VOCABULARY

Activity A   Name _____

Chapter 3   Date _____ Period _____

Complete the sentences below by writing the correct words from the chapter in the blanks.

Attitude	Memory	Tests
Concentrate	Priorities	Time
IRS Time	Procrastination	Time log
Key	Review	Time management

_____ 1. To focus your effort and attention on something is to _____.

_____ 2. Poor use of _____ is a common cause of poor study habits.

_____ 3. Do not rely on your _____ to recall important things to do.

_____ 4. _____ are rankings for things according to their importance.

_____ 5. When taking notes, listen carefully and write down the _____ points.

_____ 6. _____ means delaying or putting off decisions or activities.

_____ 7. The purpose of _____ is to measure how much you know and don't know.

_____ 8. _____ _____ is short for Individual Responsibility for Saving Time and involves taking steps to make the best use of your time.

_____ 9. After you study, take time to mentally _____ the material.

_____ 10. A written record of a person's use of time is a(n) _____ _____.

_____ 11. The planning and using of time is called _____ _____.

_____ 12. A positive _____ will help you get into your study assignment.

TIME LOG

Activity B
Chapter 3

Name _____

Date _____ Period _____

Find out how you spend your time by keeping a time log for one week. Fill in the blocks in the chart below to indicate the amount of time you spend doing each activity each day. Indicate time in hours to the nearest quarter hour (15 minutes = .25 hour; 30 minutes = .5 hour; 45 minutes = .75 hour). Remember that the total time spent for all of your combined activities should equal 24 hours each day. At the end of the week, total your time for each activity.

	Sun	Mon	Tues	Wed	Thurs	Fri	Sat	Total
Sleeping								
Eating								
Grooming								
Going to school								
Studying/Doing homework								
Working								
Doing chores								
Participating in extracurricular activities								
Watching TV/Listening to music								
Talking on the phone								
Visiting friends								
Reading and relaxing								
Doing other activities								

TIME LOG REVIEW

Activity C Name _____

Chapter 3 Date _____ Period _____

Review the time log you completed in Activity B. Then answer the questions below as you refer to the time log.

1. What activity took up the most time? _____
2. How many hours did you spend doing chores?
   a. Average hours per day: _____
   b. Total weekly hours: _____
3. How many hours did you spend doing homework and studying?
   a. Average hours per day: _____
   b. Total weekly hours: _____
4. How many hours did you spend taking part in extracurricular activities?
   a. Average hours per day: _____
   b. Total weekly hours: _____
5. How many hours did you spend working?
   a. Average hours per day: _____
   b. Total weekly hours: _____
6. How many hours did you spend watching TV and listening to music?
   a. Average hours per day: _____
   b. Total weekly hours: _____
7. How many hours did you spend reading and relaxing?
   a. Average hours per day: _____
   b. Total weekly hours: _____
8. How many hours did you spend visiting friends?
   a. Average hours per day: _____
   b. Total weekly hours: _____
9. How many hours do you usually sleep per day? _____
10. About how much time do you spend eating each day? _____
11. About how much time do you spend grooming each day? _____
12. About how many hours per day do you spend talking on the phone? _____
13. About how much total weekly time do you spend doing other activities? _____
14. Are you spending your time on your most important priorities? _____
15. When do you usually do your homework and study? Is this the best time of day for you to study?
    _____
    _____
16. Do you usually spend more time doing homework and studying or working? _____
17. Do you spend enough time studying? _____

(Continued)

Name _____

18. Do you spend enough time relaxing? _____
19. Do you spend enough time doing chores? _____
20. Which activities are taking up too much of your time? Can you reduce the time spent on these activities?
_____
_____

21. Are you usually able to complete important tasks on time? _____
22. Are you a good time manager now? _____
23. What daily habits would you like to change to improve the use of your time? _____
_____

24. What new habits can you develop to give yourself more free time? _____
_____

25. How could you use the free time gained? _____
_____

26. What steps can you take to make your study time more effective? _____
_____
_____

IRS TIME

Activity D Name _____

Chapter 3 Date _____ Period _____

Place yourself on IRS Time by filling in the following "Things to Do" list with all of the tasks you want to accomplish within the next week. Check the "A" column for tasks that you absolutely must do. Check the "B" column for tasks that you should do. Check the "C" column for tasks you want to do if you have time. Follow your list for two days, checking off tasks as you complete them. Then answer the questions at the bottom of the page.

Priority A B C	Things to Do	Completed
___ ___ ___	1. _____	___
___ ___ ___	2. _____	___
___ ___ ___	3. _____	___
___ ___ ___	4. _____	___
___ ___ ___	5. _____	___
___ ___ ___	6. _____	___
___ ___ ___	7. _____	___
___ ___ ___	8. _____	___
___ ___ ___	9. _____	___
___ ___ ___	10. _____	___
___ ___ ___	11. _____	___
___ ___ ___	12. _____	___
___ ___ ___	13. _____	___
___ ___ ___	14. _____	___
___ ___ ___	15. _____	___
___ ___ ___	16. _____	___
___ ___ ___	17. _____	___
___ ___ ___	18. _____	___
___ ___ ___	19. _____	___
___ ___ ___	20. _____	___

Do you think you are individually responsible for saving time? Explain your answer. _____
_____
_____

What steps could you take to manage your time better? _____
_____
_____

GOOD AND POOR STUDY HABITS

Activity E Name _____

Chapter 3 Date _____ Period _____

Identify each of the following study habits as being good or poor. Then in the appropriate column, write "always," "sometimes," or "never" to indicate how often you practice each habit.

GOOD HABITS	POOR HABITS	STUDY HABITS
		1. Take notes in class.
		2. Take notes when you read assignments.
		3. Study in a cluttered area.
		4. Follow directions.
		5. Gather all the supplies you need before you start to study.
		6. Study in an area where you will be distracted.
		7. Set priorities for your time.
		8. Put off big assignments until the last day.
		9. Do all your studying the night before a test.
		10. Work in an area that is quiet and relaxing.
		11. Study and review the easy parts first.
		12. Do what must be done first.
		13. Study the tough parts last.
		14. Try to do two activities at the same time.
		15. Study when you are rested.
		16. Take a few moments after you study to think about what you studied.
		17. Study while watching TV.
		18. Do a little each day on big assignments that are due in a week or more.

4 COOPERATIVE EDUCATION

REINFORCING VOCABULARY

Activity A
Chapter 4

Name _____

Date _____ Period_____

Putting one letter in each blank, write the term that belongs in each sentence below.

1. A __ __ __ __ __ __ __ __ __ __ __ employee is one that an employer can count on to perform his or her job in a satisfactory manner.

2. A(n) __ __ __ __ __ __ __ __ __ __ __ __ __ __ __ __ __ is a contract that outlines the responsibilities of everyone involved in a cooperative education work experience.

3. Working papers, working permits, or __ allow minors to be employed and set limits on the hours of work and the kinds of jobs that can be performed.

4. Local businesses cooperate with schools to employ students in part-time positions through __ __ __ __ __ __ __ __ __ __ __ __ __ __ __ __ __ __ __ programs.

5. A(n) __ __ __ __ __ __ __ __ __ __ __ __ is developed by the employer, the coordinator, and the student to state what the student will learn.

6. __ __ __ __ __ __ __-__ __ __ __ __ __ __ __ __ __ __ __ are people who supervise cooperative education programs and provide guidance to students in school and at work.

CO-OP INTERVIEW

Activity B   Name _____

Chapter 4   Date _____ Period _____

Talk with a student who is currently in a cooperative education program. Get answers to the questions listed below. If you are enrolled in a co-op program, you may wish to supply the information based on your own experiences.

Where do you work? _____

What is the title of your position? _____

What are your duties? _____
_____

How many hours do you work each day, and what days do you work each week? _____
_____

What safety regulations are you required to follow? _____
_____
_____

What special tools and equipment are needed for your job? _____
_____

What dress regulations are you required to follow? _____
_____

What skills and knowledge have you gained since beginning the co-op program? _____
_____
_____

What problems have you had in completing your work assignments? _____
_____
_____

What interesting or challenging experiences have you had with your supervisors or co-workers? _____
_____
_____

What types of classroom instruction would help you at work? _____
_____
_____

What are your career goals? _____
_____

What are your overall feelings about the co-op program? _____
_____
_____

Other information: _____
_____
_____

A SELF-EVALUATION

Activity C
Chapter 4

Name _____

Date _____ Period _____

Students in co-op programs are usually evaluated by their supervisors, but evaluating your own job performance can also be helpful. Complete the following self-evaluation. If you work, base the evaluation on your job performance. If you do not work, base the evaluation on your performance as a student. Read each statement and place a check in the appropriate column. Then list ways to improve upon your weaknesses.

Statements	Always	Usually	Sometimes	Never	Ways I Can Improve
I arrive at work on time.					
I have a good attendance record.					
I have a positive attitude.					
I am interested in my job.					
I have the knowledge and skills needed to do my job.					
I am physically able to do my job.					
I follow safety rules.					
I am honest.					
I cooperate with others.					
I work well without supervision.					
I plan ahead to do the best I can.					
I'm able to make decisions on the job.					
I try to improve when my supervisor offers suggestions.					
I do my job well.					

Other comments: _____

_____

_____

UNDERSTANDING COOPERATIVE EDUCATION

Activity D   **Name** _____

Chapter 4   **Date** _____ **Period** _____

Answer the following questions about cooperative education programs.

1. How do cooperative education jobs differ from part-time jobs students find on their own? _____

2. What does the teacher-coordinator do to help students succeed in a cooperative education program? _____

3. What information is included in a training agreement? _____

4. What is the difference between a training agreement and a training plan? _____

5. What is the purpose of an employment certificate? _____

6. Explain the employer's responsibility to pay fair wages. _____

7. How can employees show responsibility toward their jobs? _____

8. How can cooperative education students meet their school's expectations? _____

5 VOCATIONAL STUDENT ORGANIZATIONS

REINFORCING VOCABULARY

Activity A
Chapter 5

Name _____

Date _____ Period_____

Complete each of the following statements by writing the letter of the correct response in the blank.

_____ 1. A person who influences the actions of others is called a(n) _____.

_____ 2. The president, vice president, secretary, and treasurer are the _____ of a club.

_____ 3. The most common reference used in parliamentary law is _____.

_____ 4. A(n) _____ is a list of activities that will occur during a meeting.

_____ 5. _____ is an orderly way of conducting a meeting and discussing group business.

_____ 6. The person who usually conducts a group's meetings is the _____.

_____ 7. Groups that help students develop leadership skills and prepare to work in certain occupational areas are called _____.

_____ 8. The ability to lead or direct others on a course or in a direction is called _____.

_____ 9. Each _____ in an organization does a certain type of work.

_____ 10. Members of vocational organizations share interests and _____.

a. Agenda.
b. Career goals.
c. Committee.
d. Leader.
e. Leadership.
f. Officers.
g. Parliamentary procedure.
h. President.
i. Robert's Rules of Order.
j. Vocational student organizations.

LEARNING ABOUT VOCATIONAL ORGANIZATIONS

Activity B   Name _____

Chapter 5   Date _____ Period _____

The chart below lists some of the larger state and national vocational student organizations. Write a brief description of each organization and list the classes that you feel relate to each organization.

ORGANIZATION	DESCRIPTION OF ORGANIZATION	CLASSES THAT RELATE
1. Technology Student Association (TSA)		
2. Distributive Education Clubs of America (DECA)		
3. Future Business Leaders of America (FBLA)		
4. Future Farmers of America (FFA)		
5. Future Homemakers of America/Home Economics Related Occupations (FHA/HERO)		
6. Health Occupations Student Association (HOSA)		
7. Office Education Association (OEA)		
8. Business Professionals of America		

Which organizations described above interest you? Why? _____
_____
_____
_____

YOUR VOCATIONAL ORGANIZATION

Activity C   Name _____

Chapter 5   Date _____ Period _____

Research a vocational organization to which you belong or would like to join. Then answer the following questions.

1. What vocational student organizations are in your school?
   _____
   _____
   _____
   _____

2. Which vocational student organization is best suited to your interests and needs? _____
   _____

3. Write the motto of this organization. _____
   _____
   _____
   _____

4. What is the purpose of the organization? _____
   _____
   _____
   _____

5. What are the colors of the organization? What does each of the colors mean? _____
   _____
   _____
   _____
   _____
   _____

6. Describe the symbol of the organization. _____
   _____
   _____

7. What are the parts of the symbol and what do they mean? _____
   _____
   _____
   _____
   _____

8. Describe the official dress of the organization. _____
   _____
   _____
   _____
   _____

BEING A GOOD LEADER

Activity D
Chapter 5

Name _____

Date _____ Period _____

Describe how a leader could demonstrate each leadership trait listed. You may use examples from your own experiences, or you may choose to make up new examples.

1. A good leader respects other people. Example: _____
   _____
   _____

2. A good leader accepts responsibility and works within the group. Example: _____
   _____
   _____

3. A good leader gets along with others in a friendly and peaceful manner. Example: _____
   _____
   _____

4. A good leader gives praise where praise is due. Example: _____
   _____
   _____

5. A good leader communicates thoughts and feelings in a clear and understandable manner. Example:
   _____
   _____

6. A good leader is well informed on matters that concern the group. Example: _____
   _____
   _____

7. A good leader is confident and honest. Example: _____
   _____
   _____

8. A good leader is positive and excited about the group's goals. Example: _____
   _____
   _____

9. A good leader is open-minded and can help set group goals. Example: _____
   _____
   _____

10. A good leader can get the group started and keep it on track. Example: _____
    _____
    _____

6 YOUR RESOURCES, VALUES, AND GOALS

REINFORCING VOCABULARY

Activity A Name _____

Chapter 6 Date _____ Period _____

Write the terms being described in the blanks provided. Then find the terms in the word maze and circle them. (Terms are located horizontally, vertically, and diagonally in the maze.)

```
P A B S L A O G M R E T T R O H S S
T R U B M Z K O O D M R E S L L S Y
S V O Q K R S E D U T I T P A O L T
L W S F U O C F R A A O T O R I M I
A P E Y E D Y Y G R U T G K A L K L
O I I W X S A R R I M L U N S E Y A
G I T A M Z S P O N A M S C E R R N
M B I R E C D I O N M B U Q U B S O
R O L U P E R S O N A L V A L U E S
E U I A U S T I M N O N A O A I R R
T E B A R T S T I C A A M S V T E E
G B A C D S G L J Y R L D P F J P P
N Z O U E E B L A M C F V U H G L P
O M P F F R H A S O P R I A U L E Y
L E O R J E O T D Y G C M P L S U X
L R P I M T N Z O W E X N C N U O A
P E R S O N A L G O A L S G F B E J
G A U F B I T K I R E S O U R C E S
```

_____ 1. Goals that can be accomplished within a few days, weeks, or months.

_____ 2. Natural talents and the potential to learn easily and quickly.

_____ 3. The group of traits that makes each person unique.

_____ 4. Things that are important to a person in his or her daily life.

_____ 5. Any targets a person tries to reach in his or her career.

_____ 6. Aims or targets a person tries to reach or achieve.

_____ 7. Ideas, subjects, or activities that a person enjoys.

_____ 8. Things that are important to a person in his or her work.

_____ 9. All the things people have or can use to help get what they want.

_____ 10. Goals people want to achieve for themselves.

_____ 11. Goals that will take more than six months to accomplish.

_____ 12. Skills that a person has developed.

_____ 13. Beliefs, ideas, or objects that are important to a person.

CAREER INTERESTS AND ABILITIES INVENTORY

Activity B Name _____

Chapter 6 Date _____ Period _____

Your interests and abilities can lead you to a career that will be fun and exciting for you. List three of your interests or abilities that relate to each area below. Then list one job you might like based on each interest or ability.

MY INTERESTS AND ABILITIES	JOBS I MIGHT LIKE BASED ON MY INTERESTS AND ABILITIES
Hobbies 1. _____ 2. _____ 3. _____	1. _____ 2. _____ 3. _____
Leisure Activities 1. _____ 2. _____ 3. _____	1. _____ 2. _____ 3. _____
Favorite School Subjects 1. _____ 2. _____ 3. _____	1. _____ 2. _____ 3. _____
Part-time or Volunteer Work 1. _____ 2. _____ 3. _____	1. _____ 2. _____ 3. _____
Special Abilities 1. _____ 2. _____ 3. _____	1. _____ 2. _____ 3. _____

YOUR PERSONALITY TRAITS

Activity C
Chapter 6

Name _____

Date _____ Period _____

Your personality traits are among the resources that can help you choose a career you will like. Evaluate your personality traits by placing a check in the blanks near the statements that describe you.

1. _____ I like to work.
2. _____ I am trustworthy.
3. _____ I am often late to school.
4. _____ I can accept criticism willingly.
5. _____ I am sure of myself.
6. _____ I brag a lot.
7. _____ I am often early to school.
8. _____ I am always willing to help others.
9. _____ I only do things I like.
10. _____ I am almost always polite.
11. _____ I almost always ask, "What's in it for me?"
12. _____ I don't like to be told what to do.
13. _____ I am sometimes impolite.
14. _____ I do *only* what I have to do to get along.
15. _____ I like to work ahead.
16. _____ I am almost always careful to do things right.
17. _____ I am willing to work as hard as I have to.
18. _____ I need little direction to do things.
19. _____ I'd rather watch TV than go to school or work.
20. _____ I believe telling a lie is sometimes better than telling the truth.
21. _____ I don't believe I should have to work hard.
22. _____ I'm often unsure of myself and my decisions.
23. _____ I'm ambitious.
24. _____ I'm often sloppy about my appearance.
25. _____ I ignore things I don't like.
26. _____ I like responsibility.
27. _____ I like to please people.
28. _____ I am almost always neat about my appearance.
29. _____ I am often impatient with others.
30. _____ I have trouble following directions.

(Continued)

Name _____

From the list of traits you checked, identify the five that you believe are your best resources. Explain how each of these traits would be helpful in a career.

1. _____
   _____

2. _____
   _____

3. _____
   _____

4. _____
   _____

5. _____
   _____

Identify three traits you need to change, either positive traits you need to develop, or negative traits you need to change. Explain why changing each of these traits would be helpful in a career.

1. _____
   _____

2. _____
   _____

3. _____
   _____

SETTING AND REACHING GOALS

Activity D   **Name** _____

Chapter 6   **Date** _____ **Period** _____

You make things happen by setting goals and making plans for reaching them. Think about your goals by completing this activity. Your responses will not be graded.

1. List five goals you would like to accomplish within the next few months.

    a. _____

    b. _____

    c. _____

    d. _____

    e. _____

2. List five goals you would like to accomplish within the next five to ten years.

    a. _____

    b. _____

    c. _____

    d. _____

    e. _____

3. Select the one goal from each list that is most important to you. Write these two goals in the space provided. Use checks to show whether each goal is personal or professional and short-term or long-term.

Most Important Goals	Personal Goal	Professional Goal	Short-term Goal	Long-term Goal
a.				
b.				

(Continued)

Your Resources, Values, and Goals

Name _____

4. Select the one goal that is most important to you and write it as a statement. Indicate the date you want to reach this goal.

_____
_____
_____

5. Decide how you are going to reach your goal, and write out a detailed plan.

_____
_____
_____
_____
_____
_____
_____
_____
_____
_____
_____
_____

6. Follow through with your plan and make your goal happen!

REINFORCING VOCABULARY

Activity A
Chapter 7

Name _____
Date _____ Period _____

Fill in the blanks below with the correct terms. Then write your answers in the crossword puzzle.

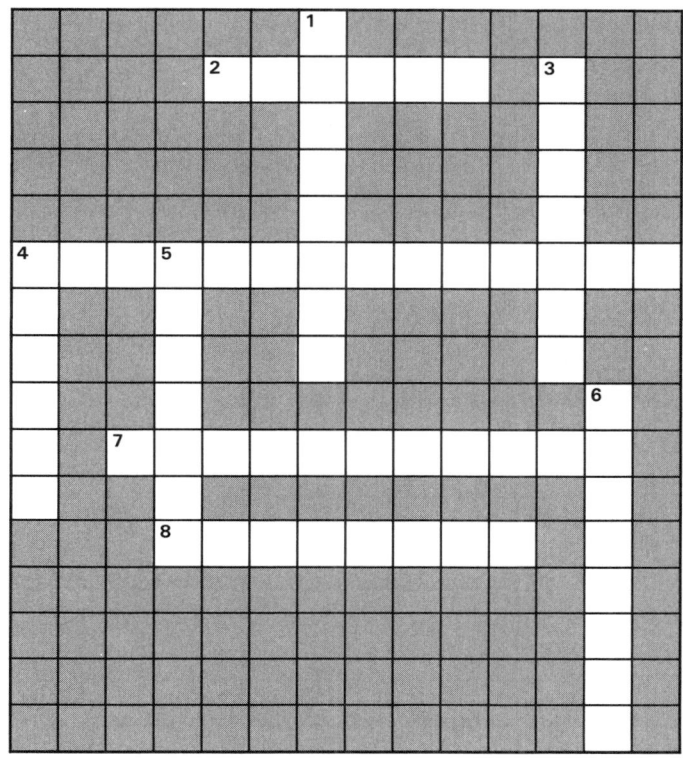

Across

_____ 2. Personal decisions may also affect _____ decisions.

_____ 4. The _____ process is the five step guide for making choices based on careful thinking and planning.

_____ 7. A(n) _____ is a choice or option when making a decision.

_____ 8. After making a decision, it is important to _____ the results.

Down

_____ 1. A(n) _____ occurs when one thing is given up in return for another.

_____ 3. Decisions that are made often and automatically are _____ decisions.

_____ 4. The first step in making a decision is to _____ the decision to be made.

_____ 5. A decision that is made based on feelings or reactions to a situation is a(n) _____ decision.

_____ 6. Making a(n) _____ means making a choice or a judgment.

Decisions 35

THE DECISION-MAKING PROCESS

Activity B Name _____

Chapter 7 Date _____ Period _____

Match the following steps in a routine decision with the correct steps in the decision-making process. Then answer the questions that follow.

_____ 1. The sweater looks great on me, but I sometimes get too warm when I wear it. The flannel shirt looks old and faded. It also fits rather snugly. The sweatshirt looks casual, but neat. It is very comfortable.

_____ 2. It turned out to be warmer today than I expected. I would have been warm in the sweater and uncomfortable in the tight flannel shirt. Wearing the sweatshirt was a good decision.

_____ 3. I will wear the sweatshirt.

_____ 4. What shall I wear to school?

_____ 5. A sweater, a flannel shirt, a sweatshirt.

a. Define the decision to be made.
b. List all possible alternatives.
c. Forecast the outcome of each alternative.
d. Make a decision and act on it.
e. Evaluate the results.

Choose one of the steps of the decision-making process. Explain what might happen if you failed to take that step when making an important decision.

_____
_____
_____
_____

When do you feel it would be most helpful to use the decision-making process? Explain your answer.

_____
_____
_____
_____

Describe any times when you feel it would not be worthwhile to use the decision-making process.

_____
_____
_____
_____

TRADE-OFFS

Activity C Name _____

Chapter 7 Date _____ Period _____

For every decision you make, there are trade-offs. Read the decisions listed below and describe one trade-off for each decision.

1. To lose ten pounds in a month. _____
   _____
   _____

2. To get a drivers license within two weeks. _____
   _____
   _____

3. To go to Europe on spring break. _____
   _____
   _____

4. To get a job immediately after graduating from high school. _____
   _____
   _____

5. To make the honor roll next grading period. _____
   _____
   _____

6. To play a video game after school. _____
   _____
   _____

7. To save $3,000 in one year for a car. _____
   _____
   _____

8. To learn to dance in four weeks. _____
   _____
   _____

9. To buy a new outfit this month. _____
   _____
   _____

10. To complete all homework in school during study hall. _____
    _____
    _____

PREPARING FOR CAREER DECISIONS

Activity D   Name _____

Chapter 7   Date _____ Period _____

Planning ahead is the key to making a satisfying career decision. By starting to think about a career now, you will be better prepared to make decisions in the future. Start planning for your career by answering the following questions.

1. What courses and programs will you take in high school? _____
   _____
   _____
   _____
   _____
   _____

2. How much effort will you put into your studies? _____
   _____
   _____
   _____
   _____

3. What skills will you develop? _____
   _____
   _____
   _____
   _____
   _____

4. What education and training beyond high school are you willing to pursue? _____
   _____
   _____

5. What careers will you explore? _____
   _____
   _____
   _____
   _____

MAKING DECISIONS AT WORK

Activity E   Name _____

Chapter 7   Date _____ Period _____

Some decisions at work are easy to make, but other decisions require more careful thought. The more you practice making those difficult decisions, the easier they will become. Read the case studies that follow and answer the questions to complete the decision-making process.

1. Jeannie has just begun a new job as an air conditioning and heating mechanic's assistant. Jeannie's job is to get the tools ready for her boss. She is also expected to clean up the work area at the end of the day. During the day, other workers ask Jeannie to go get materials for them. She helps stock supplies at the job site. Sometimes Jeannie does errands for the senior mechanics on the job.

    Jeannie's work area is often left dirty at the end of the day. Sometimes she keeps her boss from leaving work on time. She is often late in putting away the equipment. Lately her supervisor has been reprimanding her quite often. Jeannie may not get a raise at the next salary review if her work has not improved.

    a. What decision does Jeannie have to make? _____
    _____
    _____

    b. What are her alternatives? _____
    _____
    _____

    c. What are the trade-offs for each alternative? _____
    _____
    _____
    _____

    d. What is the probable outcome of each alternative? _____
    _____
    _____
    _____

    e. What decision would you make if you were in Jeannie's place? _____
    _____
    _____

    f. Why would you make this decision? _____
    _____
    _____

(Continued)

2. Henry is a senior in a cooperative education program. He has been working for four weeks as a word processor in an office. Henry is one of six cooperative education students employed by the firm. Henry has much better office skills than the other students.

   It is time for Ms. Jacobs, Henry's boss, to evaluate him and determine his continued employment. She has reviewed his file and has found that Henry does far more work than any of the other students. However, she has also noted that Henry is nearly 15 minutes late every day.

   When talking to Henry, Ms. Jacobs once asked Henry why he was late every day. Henry replied, "I do more work than any other part-time worker here. I don't think it should matter if I come in late. I get the same pay and do more work. It's not fair that I work as long as the others."

   Ms. Jacobs sees Henry's lateness as a serious problem. She is afraid that the other students will begin to come in late if Henry continues to do so. On the other hand, she sees Henry's skills as an asset to the company.

   a. What decision does Henry's boss have to make? _____

   b. What are her alternatives? _____

   c. What are the trade-offs for each alternative? _____

   d. What is the probable outcome of each alternative? _____

   e. What decision would you make if you were Henry's boss? _____

   f. Why would you make this decision? _____

8 TYPES OF CAREERS

REINFORCING VOCABULARY

Activity A
Chapter 8

Name _____

Date _____ Period _____

Match the following chapter terms with their definitions.

_____ 1. Demands that an applicant live in a certain area.

_____ 2. Often fills entry-level jobs.

_____ 3. A group of careers that are related in some way.

_____ 4. Requires experience and/or vocational training.

_____ 5. Requires a formal training program beyond high school, such as an apprenticeship, community college program, or company-sponsored training program.

a. Career cluster.
b. Residency requirement.
c. Semiskilled labor.
d. Skilled labor.
e. Unskilled labor.

Match the following career clusters discussed in the chapter with their descriptions.

_____ 1. Careers that involve moving people and freight on land, at sea, and in the air.

_____ 2. Examples of careers include actors, musicians, painters, dancers, photographers, cartoonists, stage managers, religious leaders, and historians.

_____ 3. Careers that relate to working with plants and animals.

_____ 4. Careers that involve performing tasks for customers.

_____ 5. Careers that involve production work in factories.

_____ 6. Careers that involve clerical, computer, banking, insurance, and administrative work.

_____ 7. Careers that involve building and designing roads, bridges, and buildings.

_____ 8. Careers that involve the study and use of oceans, seas, and rivers.

_____ 9. Careers in federal, state, and local governments.

_____ 10. Careers that involve the promoting, buying, selling, and delivery of goods and services.

_____ 11. Careers that relate to improving people's quality of life.

_____ 12. Careers that involve helping people enjoy themselves.

_____ 13. Careers that are concerned with forests, wildlife, air, soil, water, minerals, and chemicals.

_____ 14. Results of these careers are seen through newspapers, magazines, books, television, motion pictures, still photographs, radio, and telephone.

_____ 15. Careers that involve work in hospitals, nursing homes, doctor's and dentist's offices, and drug stores.

a. Agriculture.
b. Business and office.
c. Communication and media.
d. Construction.
e. Consumer education and home economics.
f. Fine arts and humanities.
g. Health.
h. Hospitality and recreation.
i. Manufacturing.
j. Marine science.
k. Marketing and distribution.
l. Natural resources and environment.
m. Personal services.
n. Public service.
o. Transportation.

OCCUPATIONAL RESEARCH

Activity B Name _____

Chapter 8 Date _____ Period _____

Select one occupation that interests you and answer the following questions about that occupation. Use publications, such as the *Dictionary of Occupational Titles* and the *Occupational Outlook Handbook,* as well as people for your sources of information. Share the results of your research orally in class.

1. What is the title of an occupation that interests you? _____

2. Before consulting any other resources, describe what you think people in this occupation do. _____
   _____
   _____
   _____

3. Now consult a publication on careers and describe what it says people in this occupation do. _____
   _____
   _____
   _____

4. Where do people in this occupation work? _____
   _____
   _____

5. What is the general employment outlook for this occupation in five years? _____
   In ten years? _____

6. How many people are employed in this occupation? _____

7. What local companies employ workers in this occupation? _____
   _____
   _____
   _____

8. List the major types of tools, equipment, machines, and materials used by workers in this occupation.

TOOLS	EQUIPMENT
MACHINES	**MATERIALS**

(Continued)

Name _____

9. Will you need training beyond high school for this occupation? _____ If so, what kind and amount of training will you need?

WHAT KIND OF TRAINING?	HOW MUCH TRAINING
_____ On-the-job training.	
_____ Apprenticeship.	
_____ Trade or technical school.	
_____ Community college.	
_____ College or university.	
_____ Military.	

10. List qualifications other than education that are necessary in this occupation.

Physical Qualifications: _____
_____
_____

Mental Qualifications: _____
_____
_____

Emotional Qualifications: _____
_____
_____

11. What are some similar occupations? _____
_____

12. Is the work dangerous? _____
    If so, in what way? _____
    What precautions do workers take to ensure their safety? _____
    _____

13. Is the work seasonal? _____ If so, when are peak employment periods?
    _____
    When are the off-seasons? _____
    Are layoffs common during off-seasons? _____

14. Would you have to move from the area to be employed in this occupation? ____

(Continued)

Types of Careers 43

Name _____

15. Compare your qualifications with the qualifications needed to work in this occupation.

MY QUALIFICATIONS	REQUIRED QUALIFICATIONS
_____	_____
_____	_____
_____	_____
_____	_____
_____	_____
_____	_____
_____	_____
_____	_____

How can you develop any qualifications you are lacking? _____
_____

16. Does this occupation still appeal to you? _____
    If not, why not? _____
    _____

EXPLORING CAREER CLUSTERS

Activity C   Name _____

Chapter 8   Date _____ Period _____

The 15 career clusters described in Chapter 8 are listed below. Place a check in front of the career clusters that interest you.

_____ Agriculture.

_____ Business and office.

_____ Communication and media.

_____ Construction.

_____ Consumer education and home economics.

_____ Fine arts and humanities.

_____ Health.

_____ Hospitality and recreation.

_____ Manufacturing.

_____ Marine science.

_____ Marketing and distribution.

_____ Natural resources and environment.

_____ Personal services.

_____ Public service.

_____ Transportation.

In the space below, indicate the career clusters you checked and list at least two occupations in each cluster that interest you. Explain why each occupation interests you.

Name of cluster: _____	Reasons for your interest: _____
Occupations 1. _____	_____
2. _____	_____
3. _____	_____
4. _____	_____

Name of cluster: _____	Reasons for your interest: _____
Occupations 1. _____	_____
2. _____	_____
3. _____	_____
4. _____	_____

(Continued)

Name _____

Name of cluster: _____

Occupations 1. _____

2. _____

3. _____

4. _____

Reasons for your interest: _____

_____

_____

_____

_____

Name of cluster: _____

Occupations 1. _____

2. _____

3. _____

4. _____

Reasons for your interest: _____

_____

_____

_____

_____

From all the occupations you listed, identify the two that interest you most.

Occupation 1: _____

Occupation 2: _____

List the abilities and skills needed for the occupations listed above.

Occupation 1: _____

_____

_____

Occupation 2: _____

_____

_____

Do you have the abilities and skills listed? What can you do to develop any abilities and skills you do not have?

_____

_____

_____

9 THE JOB SEARCH

REINFORCING VOCABULARY

Activity A
Chapter 9

Name _____

Date _____ Period _____

Write the terms being described in the blanks provided.

Closed ad
Job application form
Open ad
Private employment agency

Public employment service
References
Resume
Want ads

_____ 1. The names of these people who know you and can speak about your character and skills are listed on your resume.

_____ 2. This provides specific information about the job, the pay, and the company.

_____ 3. This describes your education, work experience, and other qualifications for work.

_____ 4. This government supported service helps people find jobs in and out of the government and receives no fees.

_____ 5. You will find this common source of job information in the classified section of the newspaper.

_____ 6. This gives general information about jobs, usually without giving a salary figure or mentioning the company's name.

_____ 7. This form asks for background information about you, which employers use to compare you with other candidates for a job.

_____ 8. This type of business helps people find jobs and receives a fee from either the employer or the applicant.

WANT AD ABBREVIATIONS

Activity B
Chapter 9

Name _____

Date _____ Period _____

Many want ads use abbreviations to save space. Study the abbreviations listed in Chart 9-2 on page 106 of the text. Then read each ad below and write out the entire ad without using abbreviations. Use a dictionary to look up any unfamiliar abbreviations.

1.
> Temp., p/t help wanted. No exp. nec., co. will train. Some eve. hrs., good sal., light wk. Call 555-1212.

_____
_____
_____
_____

2.
> F/T ofc. wk., oppty. to grow into mgr. position. Some bkkg. exp. nec., type 50 wpm. Call Ms. Jones between 9 a.m. and 3 p.m. at 555-6677.

_____
_____
_____
_____

3.
> Immed. opening for asst. mgr. Ex. benefits, sal. neg. Refs, & 5 yrs. exp. req. (EOE) Joe's Fast Foods, call Mr. Banks 555-6273.

_____
_____
_____
_____

USING WANT ADS

Activity C   Name _____

Chapter 9   Date _____ Period _____

Find the classified section in your local newspaper and locate the want ads. Find an ad that matches your interests and your level of education and mount it in the space below. Use the ad to answer the questions that follow.

[ ]

1. What is the title of the advertised job? _____
2. What salary is listed or expected for this job? _____
3. What education is required for this job? _____
   _____
4. What job requirements are listed? _____
   _____
   _____
5. What strengths do you possess for this job? _____
   _____
6. Whom should you contact for further information concerning this job? _____
   _____
7. What further training might you need for this job? _____
   _____
   _____
8. How can you get more information about the company before you make contact with them? _____
   _____
   _____
9. What questions should you be prepared to answer when you make contact with the company? _____
   _____
   _____
   _____
10. What will you say if you make telephone contact for more information about this job? _____
    _____
    _____

RESUME WORKSHEET

Activity D   **Name** _____

Chapter 9   **Date** _____ **Period** _____

Develop your own resume by filling in the information requested. Follow the guidelines given in the text. You may include optional information if you wish. Ask a friend or relative to read over your resume and give you suggestions. Then type or neatly print your final resume on your own paper.

Name: _____

Address: _____

Telephone number: _____

Social security number: _____

EMPLOYMENT:

_____
_____
_____
_____
_____
_____
_____

EDUCATION:

_____
_____
_____
_____
_____
_____
_____

ACTIVITIES AND HONORS:

_____
_____
_____

HOBBIES:

_____
_____

REFERENCES:

_____
_____
_____
_____

APPLYING FOR EMPLOYMENT

Activity E
Chapter 9

Name _____

Date _____ Period _____

Complete this application for employment. Print clearly and fill in all the requested information. Apply for one of the following positions:

- Clerk/typist
- Counter salesperson
- Garage mechanic
- Nursing assistant
- Greenhouse aide
- Child care aide

APPLICATION FOR EMPLOYMENT

PERSONAL INFORMATION

Name _____
       Last   First   Middle

Present Address _____
                    Street   City   State   Zip

Telephone (___) _____
              Area

JOB INTEREST

Position for which you are applying: _____

Salary desired: _____ Date you can start: _____

Have you ever been employed by this company before? _____

If yes, where? _____ When? _____

EDUCATION AND TRAINING

Name and Address of School	Number of Years Completed	Major Studies
Grade School		
High School		
Trade or Business School		
College		

EMPLOYMENT RECORD

Name and Address of Employers Beginning with Your Most Recent Employer	Type of Work	Dates Employed	Reason for Leaving

(Continued)

Name _____

If you have served in the U.S. Armed Forces, indicate:

Branch _____ Special Training _____

Rank Attained _____ Years in Service _____

Honors or Awards_____ Date of Separation_____

REFERENCES (List the names of three people not related to you whom you have known at least one year.)

Name	Address	Phone Number	Occupation	Years Known

ADDITIONAL DATA

Have you ever been convicted of a crime (other than traffic, game law, or other minor violations)? _____

If yes, explain the offense and circumstances regarding the conviction: _____

Is your age under 18? _____ Over 70? _____

Are you a U.S. citizen? _____ If no, do you have an alien registration card or valid U.S. work permit?

_____

Non-English languages you read _____ speak _____ write _____

Special skills, knowledge, and abilities that qualify you for the position you are seeking: _____

_____

_____

PHYSICAL STATUS

Are you presently or have you during the last six months been under a physician's care or in a hospital? _____

Do you have any disabilities? _____

Have you ever been compensated for, or do you currently have outstanding, a job-related injury or claim? _____

If yes to any of the above, explain: _____

_____

_____

Thank you for completing this application form and for your interest in employment with us. We would like to assure you that your opportunity for employment with this company will be based only on your merit without regard to your race, religion, sex, age, national origin, or handicaps.

PLEASE READ CAREFULLY
APPLICANT'S CERTIFICATION AND AGREEMENT

I certify that the facts contained in this application are true and complete to the best of my knowledge. I understand that, if employed, falsified statements on this application shall be grounds for dismissal.

I authorize investigation of all statements contained in this application. I authorize the references listed above to give you any and all information concerning my previous employment and any pertinent information they may have, personal or otherwise. I release all parties from all liability for any damage that may result from furnishing this information to you.

_____   _____
DATE   SIGNATURE OF APPLICANT

10 INTERVIEWS

REINFORCING VOCABULARY

Activity A   Name _____

Chapter 10   Date _____ Period _____

Match the following terms from the chapter with their correct definitions.

_____ 1. A talk between an employer and a job applicant.

_____ 2. The company representative who talks with job applicants.

_____ 3. Telephone conversation between a company representative and a job applicant.

_____ 4. Face-to-face meeting between an employer and a job applicant.

_____ 5. A job applicant or a person who is looking for a job.

_____ 6. A brief letter written in business form to thank the interviewer for the interview.

a. Follow-up letter.
b. Interview.
c. Interviewee.
d. Interviewer.
e. Personal interview.
f. Telephone interview.

Write a one- or two-paragraph story about someone who is looking for a job. Correctly use all of the above vocabulary terms in your story.

_____
_____
_____
_____
_____
_____
_____
_____
_____
_____
_____
_____
_____
_____
_____
_____
_____
_____
_____
_____

COMPANY RESEARCH

Activity B
Chapter 10

Name _____

Date _____ Period _____

Select a company at which you would like to work and a job that you would like to have. Then research the company and the job. Provide the information requested below.

1. At what company would you like to work? _____
   _____

2. Why would you like to work there? _____
   _____
   _____

3. What job would you like to have? _____

4. Why do you think you would like this job? _____
   _____
   _____

5. What skills are needed for this job? _____
   _____

6. List any needed skills you are lacking and describe how you could acquire them. _____
   _____
   _____

7. What products does the company produce, or what services does it offer? _____

8. Have you ever used these products or services? _____
   If so, were you satisfied? Explain why or why not. _____
   _____

9. How many people are employed by the company? _____

10. Does the company have plans for future growth or expansion? _____

11. What opportunities for advancement would be available to you? _____
    _____

12. List five questions you would ask if you were being interviewed for a job with this company.
    a. _____
       _____
    b. _____
       _____
    c. _____
       _____
    d. _____
       _____
    e. _____
       _____

INTERVIEW QUESTIONS

Activity C   **Name** _____

Chapter 10   **Date** _____ **Period** _____

Interviewers often ask job applicants the following questions. Answer each of the questions as though you were on a job interview. Discuss your answers in class.

1. Why do you want to work here? _____
   _____
   _____

2. Tell me about yourself. _____
   _____
   _____
   _____
   _____

3. What are your favorite subjects in school? _____
   _____

4. What are your least favorite subjects in school? _____
   _____

5. What do you like to do in your free time? _____
   _____

6. Tell me about some of your other jobs. _____
   _____
   _____
   _____

7. Why did you leave your last job? _____
   _____

8. What are your major strengths? _____
   _____
   _____

9. What are your weaknesses? _____
   _____
   _____

10. What do you want to do five years from now? _____
    _____
    _____

FOLLOW UP IN WRITING

Activity D   **Name** _____

Chapter 10   **Date** _____ **Period** _____

Bob Johnson just completed an interview for a sales position with Joseph Sebastian, personnel manager for Watson's department store. Watson's is located at 735 S. River Road in Bently, Nebraska 00923. Bob lives nearby at 832 W. Roseville Drive in Bently.

Bob had heard he should send a follow-up letter after an interview, so he wrote the letter below. Bob had the right idea, but his letter needs a little work. Read his letter and answer the questions that follow.

> Dear Joe,
> Thakns for the interview. You seem like a nice guy, and the job osunded kind of fun. I wouldn't mind working for you. Let me know if I get the job.
> Sincerely,
> Bob Johnson

What suggestions would you give Bob for improving his letter? _____

_____

_____

_____

Write a follow-up letter for Bob that might give Mr. Sebastian a better impression. (Use another sheet of paper if you need more space.)

_____

_____

_____

_____

_____

_____

_____

_____

_____

_____

_____

_____

_____

_____

_____

_____

_____

_____

_____

INTERVIEW PRACTICES

Activity E Name _____

Chapter 10 Date _____ Period _____

Listed below are a variety of interview situations. Read each situation and decide whether a good interview practice or a poor interview practice is being described. Write a G in the blank in front of a good interview practice and a P in the blank in front of a poor interview practice. If a poor interview practice is described, use the space provided to explain what the interviewee should have done differently.

_____ 1. As Glenn walked into the interviewer's office, he said, "I sure am tired. I gotta set down and have a cigarette. Ya gotta light?"

_____ 2. William arrived for his interview 15 minutes early. After giving his name to the receptionist, he quietly waited until he was called for his interview.

_____ 3. Because Jackie was babysitting her two-year-old brother, she brought him along to her interview.

_____ 4. After a fun day at the beach, Blake hurried to his interview at the drug store wearing brightly colored shorts and no shirt.

_____ 5. When Joan interviewed at Hamburger Heaven, she said, "Ya know, I've eaten your hamburgers and they're really gross."

_____ 6. When Katie interviewed for the receptionist's job, she said, "I don't have experience answering business phones, but I love talking with people and I'm willing to learn."

_____ 7. Raymond was nervous at his first job interview. He looked at the wall instead of the interviewer and gave simple yes and no answers to the questions he was asked.

_____ 8. Brian said to the interviewer, "I would do a good job as a grounds keeper for your company. For three years, I have had my own outdoor maintenance service, and all my customers have been satisfied."

_____ 9. The interviewer told Sally to make herself comfortable, so she sprawled out on the couch and began chewing bubble gum.

(Continued)

Name _____

_____ 10. Tom told the interviewer at A to Z Dry Cleaners that he and his family have always gotten excellent service there.

_____

_____

_____ 11. Melanie said to the interviewer, "I want to be a candystriper because I like helping people and would like to become a nurse."

_____

_____

_____ 12. Carla came to her interview for the typing position wearing a neatly pressed skirt and blouse.

_____

_____

_____ 13. James told the interviewer, "I'm sorry I'm late, but I overslept."

_____

_____

_____ 14. Marta said to the interviewer, "I'll take any kind of work. I don't care what I do."

_____

_____

_____ 15. Amy said to the interviewer, "What hours would I work? I sleep until noon, so I can't get to work until 1 p.m.

_____

_____

11 WINNING AT WORK
REINFORCING VOCABULARY

Activity A
Chapter 11

Name _____

Date _____ Period _____

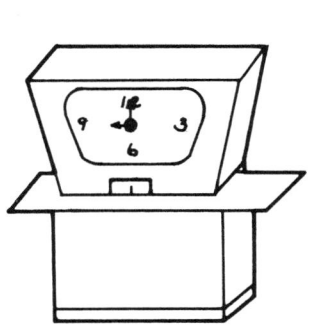
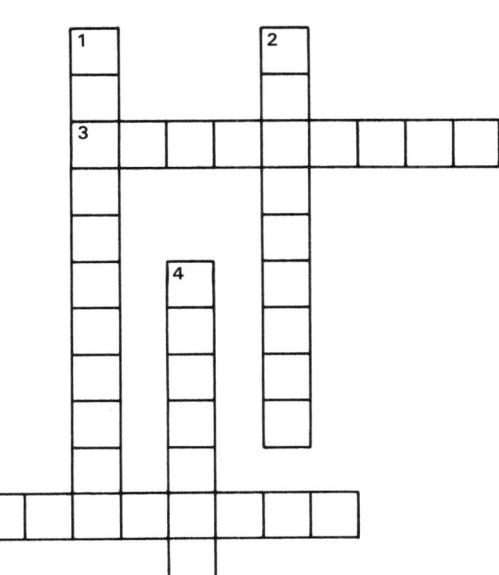

Across

3. A _____ is a severe expression of disapproval.
5. A person who is _____ comes to work on time.

Down

1. The end of employment or the loss of a job is called _____.
2. A right that is given to an employee as a benefit or favor is a _____.
4. A _____ is a loss or hardship for breaking company rules and policies.

IF YOU WERE AN EMPLOYER

Activity B Name _____

Chapter 11 Date _____ Period _____

Pretend you are the owner of a small business. Answer the following questions about the expectations you would have for your employees.

1. What type of business would you own? _____
2. What traits would you want your employees to have? _____

3. How would you expect your employees to behave toward one another? _____

4. How would you expect your employees to behave toward you? _____

5. How would you expect your employees to behave toward your customers and business contacts? _____

6. What kind of employees would you reward with raises and promotions? _____

7. What company rules and policies would you have for your employees? _____

8. What kinds of penalties would you have for employees who broke your rules and policies? _____

9. Under what circumstances would you fire an employee? _____

10. What time would you expect your employees to begin work each day? _____
11. What kinds of privileges would you extend to your employees? _____

12. Do you think your employees would enjoy working for you? Explain your answer. _____

WINNERS OR LOSERS?

Activity C   **Name** _____

Chapter 11   **Date** _____ **Period** _____

Read the case studies below and answer the questions that follow.

> Mary works as a typist for an insurance company. Mary has worked for the company for only a month. However, her boss is impressed with how quickly Mary has learned her job. She works hard and follows directions well.
>
> Yesterday, while the receptionist was on her lunch break, Mary was helping out by answering the phone. She answered a call from a policyholder asking whether Mary's company planned to increase their rates this year. Trying to be helpful, Mary looked through the receptionist's desk. She found a file labeled, "New Rates—For Company Use ONLY." Mary opened the file and quoted the new rates to the caller.

1. What are Mary's winning work traits? _____

   _____

   _____

   _____

2. What losing work traits does Mary need to improve? _____

   _____

   _____

   _____

> Robert is a stock clerk at a local grocery store. Robert is proud of his job and of the store where he works. He never shops anywhere else, and he tells all his friends to shop there, too.
>
> Robert does an excellent job of keeping the shelves of the store neat and clean and stocked with products. When Robert gets busy stocking, he doesn't like anything to interrupt him. In fact, the other day, the store manager heard Robert say to a customer, "Would you get out of my way, lady? Can't you see I'm trying to put these cans on the shelf?"

3. What are Robert's winning work traits? _____

   _____

   _____

   _____

4. What losing work traits does Robert need to improve? _____

   _____

   _____

   _____

WINNING WORK HABITS

Activity D Name _____

Chapter 11 Date _____ Period _____

As you read each of the following statements about good work habits, decide whether your work habits are "on target" with the statement or they "need improvement." Place a check in the column that best describes your work habits.

		On Target	Need Improvement
1.	I keep my work area neat and clean.	_____	_____
2.	I respect materials, tools, and equipment.	_____	_____
3.	I observe good health and safety practices.	_____	_____
4.	I report to work on time.	_____	_____
5.	I do not abuse work breaks.	_____	_____
6.	I get along with my co-workers.	_____	_____
7.	I carry out orders.	_____	_____
8.	I take pride in my work and do it to the best of my ability.	_____	_____
9.	I am eager to learn more about my job.	_____	_____
10.	I have a good attendance record.	_____	_____
11.	I don't waste time on the job.	_____	_____
12.	I am eager to help others whenever I can.	_____	_____
13.	I am courteous.	_____	_____
14.	I take pride in my personal appearance.	_____	_____
15.	I do high quality work.	_____	_____
16.	I do accurate and neat work.	_____	_____
17.	I am friendly and cheerful.	_____	_____
18.	I follow company rules and regulations.	_____	_____
19.	I control my temper.	_____	_____
20.	I am loyal to my employer.	_____	_____
21.	I do my work correctly and complete it on time.	_____	_____
22.	I appreciate privileges and do not abuse them.	_____	_____
23.	I have a good attitude.	_____	_____
24.	I make an effort to improve.	_____	_____
25.	I accept responsibility for my work.	_____	_____
	Totals	_____	_____

Describe steps you can take to improve your work habits. _____

_____

_____

_____

 # 12 BEING A TEAM PLAYER

REINFORCING VOCABULARY

Activity A   **Name** _____

Chapter 12   **Date** _____ **Period** _____

Fill in the blanks with the correct chapter terms.

    Argumentative   Ridicule
    Gossip   Rumor
    Grapevine   Sarcasm
    Job description

1. A _____ _____ explains the tasks you are to perform.   1. _____

2. _____ is the use of cutting remarks.   2. _____

3. When you _____, you tell personal information about another person.   3. _____

4. To _____ a person is to make fun of him or her.   4. _____

5. A person who disagrees with just about everything can be described as _____.   5. _____

6. A bit of information that passes from one person to another without proof of accuracy is a _____.   6. _____

7. An informal and unofficial flow of information is called a _____.   7. _____

TIPS FOR GETTING ALONG

Activity B   Name _____

Chapter 12   Date _____ Period _____

Interview three people who each work in a different occupation. Ask each person to give five important tips for getting along with co-workers. List their responses in the space provided.

Occupation of First Person: _____

Tips for Getting Along with Co-workers:

1. _____
2. _____
3. _____
4. _____
5. _____

Occupation of Second Person: _____

Tips for Getting Along with Co-workers:

1. _____
2. _____
3. _____
4. _____
5. _____

Occupation of Third Person: _____

Tips for Getting Along with Co-workers:

1. _____
2. _____
3. _____
4. _____
5. _____

Why might some of the tips you were given be similar? _____
_____

Why might some of the tips you were given be different? _____
_____
_____

Do you agree with the tips listed above? Explain your answer. _____
_____
_____

Do you disagree with any of the tips listed? Explain your answer. _____
_____
_____

STUDYING WORK ATTITUDES

Activity C   Name _____

Chapter 12   Date _____ Period _____

Carefully read each situation described below and respond to each request.

1. Pretend it is your first day on a new job. Describe what you would do to make a good impression on your co-workers and supervisors. Keep your answer in mind as you complete this activity.

   _____
   _____
   _____

2. Now consider David, a stock clerk in a large supermarket. David does only what he is told to do, no more and no less. Does David have a good attitude toward work? Why or why not?

   _____
   _____
   _____

3. One day, one of David's co-workers knocked over a product display. Boxes were scattered all over the floor. At the time, David was working nearby. If you were David, what would you have done in this situation?

   _____
   _____
   _____
   _____

4. David ignored his co-worker's problem. He left his work station to tell others what had happened. David made a big joke at his co-worker's expense. If you were David's supervisor, what would you have said to David?

   _____
   _____
   _____

5. If you were the worker who knocked over the display, what would you have said to David?

   _____
   _____
   _____

6. Later the same day, David was stocking shelves. The product he was stocking belonged in another part of the store. A co-worker trying to help David told him he was making a mistake. However, David insisted he was right and started an argument. Was David correct in arguing with his co-worker?

   _____

7. What do you think David should have done?

   _____
   _____
   _____

(Continued)

Name _____

8. Before David went home that night, he overhead part of a conversation between two co-workers and their supervisor. The next morning, David told everyone what he had heard. The entire supermarket was soon talking about David and the co-workers. Was David correct in telling his co-workers about what he had overheard? Why or why not?

_____
_____
_____

9. When David's supervisor found out what had happened, he called David into his office for a conference. What do you think he said to David?

_____
_____
_____

10. If you were one of David's co-workers, what advice would you give to David?

_____
_____
_____

11. If you were David's supervisor, would you want to have David working for you? Why or why not?

_____
_____
_____

GOOD WORK HABITS IN ACTION

Activity D Name _____
Chapter 12 Date _____ Period _____

In your own words, explain how having the work habits listed below can help you get along with your co-workers. Give a specific example of how you could put each work habit into action.

1. Be friendly: _____
   _____

   Example: _____
   _____

2. Respect your co-workers: _____
   _____

   Example: _____
   _____

3. Look at your co-workers' good sides: _____
   _____

   Example: _____
   _____

4. Don't be self-centered: _____
   _____

   Example: _____
   _____

5. Don't be a know-it-all: _____
   _____

   Example: _____
   _____

6. Accept criticism positively: _____
   _____

   Example: _____
   _____

(Continued)

Name _____

7. Have a positive attitude: _____
_____
_____

   Example: _____
   _____

8. Keep a good sense of humor: _____
   _____
   _____

   Example: _____
   _____

9. Avoid the poor use of humor: _____
   _____
   _____

   Example: _____
   _____

10. Do not cause arguments: _____
    _____
    _____

    Example: _____
    _____

11. Do not spread rumors: _____
    _____
    _____

    Example: _____
    _____

12. Avoid comparisons: _____
    _____
    _____

    Example: _____
    _____

13 CHANGES IN JOB STATUS

REINFORCING VOCABULARY

Activity A
Chapter 13

Name _____
Date _____ Period _____

Match the following chapter terms and definitions.

_____ 1. Payment 1 1/2 or 2 times the regular wage that is given for hours worked beyond the normal 40-hour work week.

_____ 2. A percentage of the dollar amount of sales made.

_____ 3. A move up to a higher position within a company.

_____ 4. A set amount of money that is earned for a full year of work.

_____ 5. Being dismissed from a job for a reason beyond a worker's control, such as a cutback on production.

_____ 6. A letter written to inform an employer that an employee is quitting his or her job.

_____ 7. A set amount of money that is earned for every hour of work.

_____ 8. Extra financial rewards that are given in addition to regular paychecks.

_____ 9. Being dismissed from a job due to poor performance or the inability to get along with others.

a. Commission.
b. Fired.
c. Fringe benefits.
d. Laid off.
e. Letter of resignation.
f. Overtime pay.
g. Promotion.
h. Salary.
i. Wages.

STARTING FULL-TIME WORK

Activity B   **Name** _____

Chapter 13   **Date** _____ **Period** _____

Interview someone you know who has recently changed from part-time to full-time work. Record his or her answers to the questions that follow. Share what you learn with others in class.

1. What caused you to change from part-time to full-time work? _____
_____
_____
_____

2. What do you like most about working full-time? _____
_____
_____
_____

3. What challenged you most when you first began working full-time? _____
_____
_____
_____

4. What changes surprised you when you became a full-time worker? _____
_____
_____
_____

5. How does your lifestyle differ from when you were working part-time? _____
_____
_____
_____

6. What advice would you give to someone preparing to change from part-time work to full-time work?
_____
_____
_____
_____
_____

OTHER NOTES:
_____
_____
_____
_____
_____

CHANGING JOBS

Activity C Name _____
Chapter 13 Date _____ Period _____

The statements listed below are possible advantages and disadvantages of changing jobs. Place an A before each advantage and a D before each disadvantage. Break up into small groups to compare your answers with others in your group.

_____ 1. A new job is a chance for a new beginning.

_____ 2. A new job is a chance for growth and promotion.

_____ 3. You may have to move.

_____ 4. You may earn a higher salary.

_____ 5. You may have opportunities for retraining or advanced learning.

_____ 6. You may be labeled a "job hopper."

_____ 7. You will have new experiences and face new challenges.

_____ 8. You may lose accumulated paid sick leave.

_____ 9. You may have to rebuild vacation time.

_____ 10. You may receive better fringe benefits.

_____ 11. You will be dealing with many unknowns.

_____ 12. You may be able to travel.

_____ 13. You will have the chance to build new friendships.

_____ 14. You may have to leave a job that you like.

_____ 15. You may lose seniority rights.

_____ 16. You may not receive as many fringe benefits as in your present job.

_____ 17. You may spend less time commuting to work.

_____ 18. You may be the lowest ranked person in the new job.

LEAVING A JOB

Activity D Name _____

Chapter 13 Date _____ Period _____

Read the letter of resignation written by Joe Left and answer the questions that follow.

> 49 Crooked Road
> Alsip, IL 60658
> September 11, 19xx
>
> Mr. Bruce Kovacs
> The Music Store
> 100 Harmony Road
> Alsip, IL 60658
>
> Dear Mr. Kovacs:
>
> I will be leaving at the end of this week. I have a much better job with Stereo-Recorder Company. You should have given me that raise I asked for yesterday. This wasn't such a great job, and I'm not sorry to leave.
>
> Sincerely,
>
> *Joe Left*
> Joe Left

1. Did Joe give notice of his resignation far enough in advance? If not, how much notice should Joe have given? _____

2. Is it acceptable for Joe to tell his employer that he has a better position? Explain why or why not. _____

3. Should Joe have made the statement about the raise he didn't get? Explain why or why not. _____

4. Explain what is wrong with Joe's last statement. _____

On your own paper, rewrite Joe's letter to be more positive.

JOB CHANGES THROUGH A CAREER

Activity E
Chapter 13

Name _____

Date _____ Period _____

Read the following case study about the various job changes experienced by one worker during his career. Answer the questions related to the case.

After graduating from college, Allen got a job as a technical writer with a small company. Allen had been working for the company for about a year when it was purchased by a major corporation. When the new owners reorganized the business, Allen was laid off.

1. What positive action could Allen have taken after losing his job? _____
   _____
   _____
   _____

Allen began a new job search and found a job as a laboratory assistant in a large company. Allen enjoyed his job, but he wanted to do more. He wanted to be promoted into the research and development group.

2. How could Allen prepare for the promotion he wanted? _____
   _____
   _____
   _____

Allen got his promotion and started working as part of a team to come up with new product ideas. However, after four years, Allen is starting to think about changing jobs.

3. Why might Allen be thinking about changing jobs? _____
   _____
   _____
   _____

4. What are some questions Allen should ask himself before making a decision to change jobs? _____
   _____
   _____
   _____

5. Once Allen decides for sure that he wants to change jobs, what should he do? _____
   _____
   _____
   _____

REPORT ON CHANGES

Activity F   **Name** _____

Chapter 13   **Date** _____ **Period** _____

Read an article in a current magazine on one of the following topics:
- How to prepare for promotions.
- What to do when you lose a job.
- Why people change jobs.
- Any other topic related to changes in job status.

Write a report on the article and then report orally to the class. Be prepared to answer questions about the article.

Article title: _____

Author: _____

Source: _____

Report:

_____
_____
_____
_____
_____
_____
_____
_____
_____
_____
_____
_____
_____
_____
_____
_____
_____
_____
_____
_____
_____
_____
_____
_____
_____
_____

14 BASIC SKILLS
REINFORCING VOCABULARY

Activity A
Chapter 14

Name _____
Date _____ Period _____

Match the following words from the chapter with their definitions.

_____ 1. Metric unit of weight which is less than one ounce.

_____ 2. To read something and mark any errors found in it.

_____ 3. The group of words you know and use.

_____ 4. Metric unit that measures volume and is a little more than a quart.

_____ 5. Word that describes a person who does not know how to read or write.

_____ 6. A decimal system of weights and measures which is used by many countries.

_____ 7. Metric unit which measures distance and is just a bit longer than one yard.

_____ 8. Metric unit for measuring temperature which is a little more than two degrees Fahrenheit.

a. Celsius degrees.
b. Gram.
c. Illiterate.
d. Proofread.
e. Liter.
f. Meter.
g. Metric system.
h. Vocabulary.

STRENGTHENING YOUR VOCABULARY

Activity B Name _____

Chapter 14 Date _____ Period _____

Read the following article. List any words in the article with which you are unfamiliar in the space that follows. Look these words up in a dictionary and write their definitions.

    Dietitians have determined that limiting your intake of fats can help reduce your risk of atherosclerosis. They recommend that no more than 30 percent of your daily caloric intake come from fats. The average adult woman needs about 2000 Calories each day. This means that no more than 600 of those Calories should come from fat. The average adult man needs about 2700 Calories each day. A man, therefore, should limit his daily fat intake to 810 Calories.

    Nutrition labels on food can help you analyze how much fat you are eating. Nutrition labels list the number of grams of fat in a serving of food. Each gram of fat equals nine Calories. Therefore, using the recommendations above, the average woman should eat no more than 67 grams of fat per day. The average man should eat no more than 90 grams of fat.

    What kinds of foods are high in fats? Whole milk dairy products, choice grade meats, and desserts are some of the biggest culprits. One cup of whole milk contains eight grams of fat. A three-ounce piece of chuck roast may contain 26 grams of fat. A piece of cheesecake has about 18 grams of fat.

    Don't let these figures make you too apprehensive. You can always fill up on fruits and vegetables! Foods like apples, oranges, carrots, and peas contain only traces of fat, and they are full of vitamins, minerals, and fiber.

    Words   Definitions

1. _____ – _____
   _____

2. _____ – _____
   _____

3. _____ – _____
   _____

4. _____ – _____
   _____

5. _____ – _____
   _____

PROOFREADING FOR ACCURACY

Activity C Name _____

Chapter 14 Date _____ Period _____

Proofread the following sentences. Mark any grammar, spelling, or punctuation errors you find. Then rewrite the sentences correctly. The first sentence has been done for you.

1. When the dog tarcks mud into the house Mrs carson gets angry.
   When the dog tracks mud into the house, Mrs. Carson gets angry.

2. When a student does not do their homework, they are given a detention.
   _____

3. Running, swimming, and bicycles are good forms of exersize.
   _____

4. "Stop! she yelled.
   _____

5. A cat will clean itself by licking it's fir.
   _____

6. Clarence and Jim knows about the surprise there teacher has for the class.
   _____

7. The room was pink and and green.
   _____

8. He wont go no matter how many times you ask him.
   _____

9. The project was due Tuesday march 27.
   _____

10. Your going to the store after work, aren't you.
    _____

Basic Skills 77

MATH PRACTICE

Activity D
Chapter 14

Name _____

Date _____ Period _____

Practice using your math skills by solving the following problems. Do not use a calculator.

1.   25
      73
      12
   + 6

2.   39.5
  + 6.2

3. 1/3 + 1/7 =

4.   943
 − 21

5.   9.03
 − .72

6. 5/12 − 1/4 =

7.   886
 × 62

8.   7.2
 × 5.9

9. 1/3 × 1/2

10. 52 $\overline{)1144}$

11. .5 $\overline{)10.45}$

12. 3/8 ÷ 2 =

13. Write .66 as a percentage.

14. Write 91% as a decimal.

15. Suppose you, as a cashier, are given a five dollar bill for a $3.52 purchase. What coins and bills should you return to the customer?

16. Suppose you, as a cashier, are given a $20 bill for a $16.71 purchase. What coins and bills should you return to the customer?

17. Suppose you as a cashier are given a $20 bill and a $10 bill for a $22.43 purchase. What coins and bills should you return to the customer?

18. Convert 6 inches to centimeters.

19. Convert 52 kilograms to pounds.

20. Convert 13 gallons to liters.

15 COMMUNICATION

REINFORCING VOCABULARY

Activity A
Chapter 15

Name _____
Date _____ Period_____

Write the correct terms from the chapter in the blanks. Then fill in the crossword puzzle.

Across

5. _____ _____ is a form of nonverbal communication in which messages are sent through body movements, facial expressions, and hand gestures.
8. _____ communication is communication involving the use of words.
9. To share ideas, feelings, or information is to _____.
11. The complete name and address of a person to whom a business letter is being sent is the _____ address.
12. The _____ close is a phrase, such as "Sincerely," or "Yours truly," placed at the end of a letter.

Down

1. Making speeches before audiences is known as _____ speaking.
2. The greeting at the beginning of a letter is also known as the _____.
3. The _____ goes just above the typed name at the end of a business letter.
4. _____ communication is the sending and receiving of messages without the use of words.
6. A short statement used to tell an audience what the topic of a speech will be is an _____.
7. _____ is the return of information to the sender in order to check its accuracy.
10. A performer who tells a story using only body movements and facial expressions is called a _____.

Communication 79

SPEECH EVALUATION

Activity B   Name _____

Chapter 15   Date _____ Period _____

Using your own paper, write a speech on one of your favorite topics. A hobby, an interest, or a personal experience would be a good topic. Plan to have your speech last one to two minutes. Write notes for your speech on note cards and use them as you give your speech to the class.

Use the first form below to evaluate one of your classmates as he or she gives a speech. Circle the number on the rating scale that best describes the person in the categories listed. Write other comments at the bottom of the form. Give the completed form to your teacher, who will give it to the person you evaluated. Do not write your name on the evaluation.

Use the second evaluation form to evaluate your own speech. Summarize the helpful comments you received and use them to plan your next speech.

Evaluation of: _____

Topic of speech: _____

	Poor	Fair	Good	Very Good	Excellent
Had well-organized information:	1	2	3	4	5
Appeared calm and confident:	1	2	3	4	5
Showed enthusiasm:	1	2	3	4	5
Used proper grammar:	1	2	3	4	5
Spoke clearly:	1	2	3	4	5
Used varied tone of voice:	1	2	3	4	5
Spoke at good volume:	1	2	3	4	5
Spoke at good speed:	1	2	3	4	5
Kept good eye contact:	1	2	3	4	5
Had good posture:	1	2	3	4	5

Positive remarks: _____

Things to improve next time: _____

Evaluation of: _____

Topic of speech: _____

	Poor	Fair	Good	Very Good	Excellent
Had well-organized information:	1	2	3	4	5
Appeared calm and confident:	1	2	3	4	5
Showed enthusiasm:	1	2	3	4	5
Used proper grammar:	1	2	3	4	5
Spoke clearly:	1	2	3	4	5
Used varied tone of voice:	1	2	3	4	5
Spoke at good volume:	1	2	3	4	5
Spoke at good speed:	1	2	3	4	5
Kept good eye contact:	1	2	3	4	5
Had good posture:	1	2	3	4	5

Positive remarks: _____

Things to improve next time: _____

Copyright Goodheart-Willcox Co., Inc.

TELEPHONE PRACTICE

Activity C   **Name** _____

Chapter 15   **Date** _____ **Period** _____

Practice your telephone skills by completing the following exercises.

I. Receiving a Call

Pretend that it is 12:10 p.m. on January 6 and you are in charge of answering the telephone at work. The caller, Bill Russell of Briswell Corporation, asks to speak with Maria Romero. Maria is on her lunch break. The caller wants to check on an order he placed two weeks ago. His number is (609) 555-2232. Bill would like Maria to call him back. Use the form below to record this message.

```
To _____
Time _____   Date _____

WHILE YOU WERE   [OUT]

M _____
of _____
Phone No. _____

☐ Telephoned      ☐ Please call back
☐ Came to see you ☐ Will call again
☐ Left the following message:
_____
_____
_____
```

II. Placing an Order

Imagine that you work for Baxter Ford and your boss has asked you to call Bob Jensen at A to Z Parts Warehouse, (201) 555-0010, to place an order. You want three chrome handles for a 1986 Ford (part number A-1562-C) and two rear seat speaker grills in black plastic (part number A-1378-BF). Your work phone number is (201) 555-1292. Your work address is 5937 Kingston Drive, Northern Springs, IN 52392. Plan your call by answering the following questions.

1. What company do you represent? _____

2. Who are you calling? _____

3. What telephone number are you calling? _____

(Continued)

Name _____

4. Why are you calling? _____
_____

5. What parts are you ordering?

Part Description	Part Number	Color	Quantity
1.			
2.			

III. Making an Emergency Call

Pretend that you work for Goodman Office Supplies, located at the corner of Brice and Bethel. One of the workers, Arnie Potter, just tripped over some boxes in the warehouse. He is laying on the floor, moaning in pain, and holding his leg. Arnie is in his early 50's. He is in generally good health, but you know he suffers from high blood pressure. Role play your telephone conversation for the class as you call for an ambulance.

Complete the following chart with the emergency phone numbers your family should have. Post a copy of this list near each phone in your home.

EMERGENCY PHONE NUMBERS

Fire _____

Ambulance _____

Gas Company _____

Police _____

Doctor _____

Electric Company _____

State Police _____

Poison Control Center _____

Water Company _____

Other Emergency Numbers

_____   _____

_____   _____

Remember, if you do not know what number to call in case of an emergency, just dial the operator.

WRITING BUSINESS LETTERS

Activity D

Chapter 15

Name _____

Date _____ Period _____

Imagine that you work for Edwards & Frederickson Financial Services. Your offices are located at 144 Grand Avenue, Centerville, NJ 08701. Your boss has asked you to help gather information about a new computer system. You are to write to Mr. Alvin J. Grant, president of Grant's Computer Company, 11 Lee Avenue, Southtown, NJ 04532, to request information about the new model BRX-527 computer system. You also need information about types of software packages available and which ones would work best in your office. Write your letter in the space below following the business letter format illustrated in the text.

UNDERSTANDING BODY LANGUAGE

Activity E　　　　　　　　Name _____

Chapter 15　　　　　　　　Date _____ Period _____

Based on your first impression, write down what you think each example of body language communicates. Then draw or describe three more examples of body language and tell what each communicates. Discuss your thoughts with others in class.

1. _____

2. _____

3. _____

4. _____

5. _____

6. _____

7. _____

8. _____

9. _____

10. _____

84　　　　　　　　　　　　　　　　Copyright Goodheart-Willcox Co., Inc.

16 APPEARANCE AND CLOTHING

REINFORCING VOCABULARY

Activity A
Chapter 16

Name _____
Date _____ Period _____

Match the following chapter terms and definitions.

_____ 1. Items that are popular for only a short period of time.

_____ 2. A skin disorder caused by inflammation of the skin glands and hair follicles.

_____ 3. Cleaning and caring for your body and clothes.

_____ 4. Items like shoes, handbags, belts, neckties, and jewelry that are needed to complete outfits.

_____ 5. A set of clothing rules that employees must follow.

_____ 6. A list of all the clothes and accessories you have in your closet and drawers.

a. Accessories.
b. Acne.
c. Dress code.
d. Fads.
e. Grooming.
f. Wardrobe inventory.

In the space below, write a paragraph or two about someone who is getting ready for work. Correctly use all of the chapter terms listed above.

_____
_____
_____
_____
_____
_____
_____
_____
_____
_____
_____
_____
_____
_____
_____
_____
_____
_____
_____
_____

Copyright Goodheart-Willcox Co., Inc.

Appearance and Clothing 85

CHECK YOUR GROOMING HABITS

Activity B   Name _____

Chapter 16   Date _____ Period _____

Answer the following questions by placing a check in the column that best describes your grooming habits.

	Always	Usually	Sometimes	Never
1. Do you keep your hair neat and clean?				
2. Do you shower or bathe daily?				
3. Do you use a deodorant or antiperspirant daily?				
4. Are your nails clean and well manicured?				
5. Do you brush and floss your teeth regularly?				
6. If you wear makeup, is it applied lightly for a natural look?				
7. If you wear fragrance, is it light and pleasant?				
8. Do you wear appropriate clothing to school?				
9. Do you wear appropriate clothing to work?				
10. If you wear jewelry, does it accent your clothing?				
11. Do your accessories coordinate with your clothing?				
12. Does your clothing fit properly?				
13. Do you wear clean clothing?				
14. Is your clothing free from wrinkles?				
15. Are your shoes clean or shined?				

What can you do to improve your grooming habits? _____

_____

_____

_____

WHAT WORKERS WEAR

Activity C Name _____

Chapter 16 Date _____ Period _____

Make a list of all the clothing that you feel would be appropriate for each of the following workers.

Farm worker:
_____
_____
_____
_____

Construction worker:
_____
_____
_____
_____

Secretary:
_____
_____
_____
_____

Insurance salesperson:
_____
_____
_____
_____

Department store clerk:
_____
_____
_____
_____

Janitor:
_____
_____
_____
_____

List six occupations requiring a uniform.
_____
_____
_____

_____
_____
_____

List six occupations for which your school clothes would be suitable.
_____
_____
_____

_____
_____
_____

WARDROBE PLANNING FOR WORK

Activity D Name _____

Chapter 16 Date _____ Period _____

You get the most from your clothing dollar when you carefully plan your wardrobe. Begin planning by making a list of clothes you own that fit into each of the categories listed. Then make a complete list of the clothes you need for work. If you do not work now, make a list of clothing needs for a job you would like to have. Check to see if some of these clothing needs are met by clothing from other categories. Then make a final list of clothing to buy for work.

School Clothes	Casual Clothes	Dressy Clothes

My job: _____

Work Clothes I Need	Work Clothes I Will Buy

HEALTH
REINFORCING VOCABULARY

Activity A
Chapter 17

Name _____

Date _____ Period _____

Fill in the blanks with the correct chapter terms and find the terms in the word maze. (Terms are located forward, backward, horizontally, vertically, and diagonally in the maze.)

```
S  P  H  Y  S  I  C  A  L  F  I  T  N  E  S  S
M  T  A  D  G  H  A  A  S  M  P  H  O  E  Y  K
M  O  N  K  O  S  K  A  B  B  R  E  S  Y  M  O
E  C  H  E  N  I  O  G  P  H  Y  U  S  T  U  N
A  C  J  I  I  N  U  C  I  T  B  U  S  A  B  A
R  O  D  P  N  R  R  I  F  A  P  P  E  M  E  Z
R  G  O  E  D  M  T  K  G  E  O  U  R  L  T  A
K  U  R  C  V  A  P  U  P  S  Q  U  T  T  Y  E
O  A  F  R  A  P  R  H  N  C  O  V  S  N  A  X
G  C  D  O  E  D  U  S  T  E  E  P  R  A  E  W
O  T  E  I  D  D  E  C  N  A  L  A  B  E  T  T
```

_____ 1. A term that describes the reckless use of drugs is _____.

_____ 2. _____ is a feeling of tension, strain, or pressure.

_____ 3. _____ are chemical substances in foods that nourish the body.

_____ 4. An intake of food that supplies all the needed nutrients in the amounts needed to maintain good health is called a(n) _____.

_____ 5. A(n) _____ is any chemical substance that brings about physical, emotional, or mental changes in people.

_____ 6. _____ _____ is the ability to perform daily tasks easily with enough reserve energy to respond to unexpected demands.

A BALANCED DIET

Activity B Name _____

Chapter 17 Date _____ Period _____

Make a list of the foods you like or would like to try in each of the four food groups listed below. Then create sample menus for one day based on those foods. Be sure to include two or more servings from the meat and meat alternates group, four or more servings from the fruits and vegetables group, four or more servings from the breads and cereals group, and four or more servings from the milk and milk products group in your sample menus.

Meat and Meat Alternates	Fruits and Vegetables
Breads and Cereals	**Milk and Milk Products**

	SAMPLE DAILY MENUS	
Breakfast	Lunch	Dinner

LEARNING ABOUT STRESS

Activity C   Name _____

Chapter 17   Date _____ Period _____

Answer the following questions about how you view stress. Then, working in small groups, share your thoughts with others.

1. Place a check in the blank in front of each activity or situation you consider stressful.
   - _____ a. Going swimming.
   - _____ b. Going on your first date.
   - _____ c. Having a job interview.
   - _____ d. Taking your driver's test.
   - _____ e. Giving a speech.
   - _____ f. Moving to a different town.
   - _____ g. Playing softball.
   - _____ h. Going on a picnic.
   - _____ i. Starting a new job.
   - _____ j. Reading a book.
   - _____ k. Placing an order by telephone.
   - _____ l. Training a new person at work.
   - _____ m. Taking a surprise quiz.

2. List three more activities you consider stressful.
   - a. _____
   - b. _____
   - c. _____

3. Place a check in the blank in front of each activity or situation that you feel helps reduce stress.
   - _____ a. Taking part in physical activities like jogging, bicycling, and swimming.
   - _____ b. Having good eating and sleeping habits.
   - _____ c. Drinking lots of coffee and other drinks that contain caffeine.
   - _____ d. Talking to someone about your problems.
   - _____ e. Complaining about your problems.
   - _____ f. Trying to get away from it all for a few minutes.
   - _____ g. Planning the use of your time.
   - _____ h. Being involved in civic or social groups.
   - _____ i. Reading a book.
   - _____ j. Playing a game.
   - _____ k. Listening to music.

4. List three of your own ideas for reducing stress.
   - a. _____
   - b. _____
   - c. _____

AVOIDING SUBSTANCE ABUSE AT WORK

Activity D   **Name** _____

Chapter 17   **Date** _____ **Period** _____

Pretend you are an employer. Answer the following questions related to tobacco, alcohol, and drug use in your company.

1. What would your employee handbook say regarding your policy on smoking? _____
   _____
   _____
   _____

2. What would be the advantages of having a smoke-free workplace? _____
   _____
   _____
   _____

3. How would you help an employee who wanted to quit smoking? _____
   _____
   _____
   _____

4. What would your employee handbook say regarding your drug and alcohol policy? _____
   _____
   _____
   _____

5. What would be the advantages of having an alcohol- and drug-free workplace? _____
   _____
   _____
   _____

6. How would you help an employee who had an alcohol or drug problem? _____
   _____
   _____
   _____
   _____

18 SAFETY ON THE JOB

REINFORCING VOCABULARY

Activity A
Chapter 18

Name _____
Date _____ Period _____

Match the following chapter terms to their definitions.

_____ 1. Insurance against work-related accidents.

_____ 2. A liquid that can easily ignite and burn rapidly.

_____ 3. Oxygen, fuel, and heat: the three items that must be present for a fire to take place.

_____ 4. Describes a plug that has an electrical connection with the earth to prevent shock.

_____ 5. A national act that calls for safe and healthy working conditions; also the title of a government agency.

_____ 6. To empty or vacate a place in an organized manner for protection.

_____ 7. Immediate, temporary treatment given in the event of an accident or sudden illness.

_____ 8. A temporary or permanent physical or mental condition that prevents an employee from working.

a. Disability.
b. Evacuate.
c. Fire triangle.
d. First aid.
e. Flammable liquid.
f. Grounded.
g. OSHA.
h. Workers' compensation.

PREVENTING ACCIDENTS

Activity B   Name _____

Chapter 18   Date _____ Period _____

Select six of the occupations listed below and write them in the chart. For each occupation you select, describe an accident that could occur. Then list what could be done to prevent the accident.

Chef	Fire fighter	Pilot
Sales clerk	Plumber	Truck driver
Secretary	Electrician	Farmer
Nurse's aide	Florist	Bookkeeper
Gas station attendant	Mason	Painter
Police officer	Flight attendant	Baggage handler

OCCUPATION	POSSIBLE ACCIDENT	PREVENTIVE MEASURE
1.		
2.		
3.		
4.		
5.		
6.		

UNDERSTANDING SAFETY PRACTICES

Activity C **Name** _____

Chapter 18 **Date** _____ **Period** _____

Answer the following questions about safety on the job using the information provided in the chapter.

1. What should you do if you are not sure how to perform any part of your job? _____
   _____

2. Why might someone who is showing off be a hazard in the workplace? _____
   _____
   _____

3. How can open desk or file drawers be a hazard in an office? _____
   _____
   _____

4. Why shouldn't electrical machines or connections be touched with wet hands? _____
   _____

5. Why should office workers avoid leaning too far back in their chairs? _____
   _____

6. Why should worn electrical cords or plugs be replaced? _____
   _____
   _____

7. Why should electrical connections not be unplugged by pulling the cord? _____
   _____

8. Why should electrical circuits not be overloaded with too many machines or appliances? _____
   _____

9. When working with machinery, why should clothes fit snugly? _____
   _____

10. Explain what type of shoes should be worn on industrial or construction work sites. _____
    _____

11. What six things should a smart worker know about lifting properly? _____
    _____
    _____

12. Why should safety goggles be worn when using electrical tools and equipment? _____
    _____

13. How should an object be lifted from the floor? _____
    _____
    _____

(Continued)

Name _____

14. What types of accidents can occur in cluttered and messy work areas? _____
_____
_____

15. What safety devices should be used when mopping a floor? _____
_____
_____

16. Why should metal ladders not be used near electrical equipment or high-voltage wires? _____
_____

17. How close to your work should you position a ladder? _____
_____
_____

18. What two hazards cause nearly half of all fires each year? _____
_____
_____

19. Why should oily rags and paper never be stored in open containers? _____
_____
_____

20. What is the correct way to use the telephone to report a fire? _____
_____
_____

21. What may happen if workers fail to wash their hands before eating or smoking? _____
_____

22. Why should you stop working if you become ill on the job? _____
_____
_____

23. What should you do if you become injured on the job? _____
_____
_____

24. When giving first aid, why should you check to see that an injured person does not have anything in his or her mouth or throat? _____
_____

25. Why was the Occupational Safety and Health Act passed? _____
_____
_____

26. Why must employers place the OSHA poster in the workplace? _____
_____
_____

27. What will workers' compensation cover if a worker is injured on the job? _____
_____

19 PAYCHECKS AND TAXES

REINFORCING VOCABULARY

Activity A
Chapter 19

Name _____
Date _____ Period _____

Match the following chapter terms and definitions.

_____ 1. The total amount of money earned during a pay period.

_____ 2. Amounts of money subtracted from your gross pay.

_____ 3. The amount of money left after all deductions have been taken from your gross pay.

_____ 4. The form new employees fill out to determine how much of their pay will be withheld for taxes.

_____ 5. The form that shows the wages an employer paid you in the previous year.

_____ 6. The agency that enforces tax laws and collects taxes.

_____ 7. Indicates deductions for Social Security taxes on your paycheck.

_____ 8. A check of your tax return made by the government.

_____ 9. A length of time for which an employee's wages are calculated.

_____ 10. Someone who relies on a taxpayer for financial support, such as a child or a nonworking adult.

a. Audit.
b. Deductions.
c. Dependent.
d. FICA.
e. Gross pay.
f. IRS.
g. Net pay.
h. Pay period.
i. W-2 form.
j. W-4 form.

COMPLETING A TAX RETURN

Activity B Name _____

Chapter 19 Date _____ Period _____

You are going to prepare Robert Jackson's tax return. Use the following information, Robert's W-2 form, and the tax table below to complete the form 1040EZ on the next page.

- Robert wants $1.00 to go to the Presidential Election Campaign Fund.
- Robert's taxable interest income is $100.00.
- No one else can claim Robert on a tax return.

1 Control number		OMB No. 1545-0008					
2 Employer's name, address, and ZIP code Brookline Insurance Co. 3598 E. Division St. North Spring, IL 68253			6 Statutory employee ☐ Deceased ☐ Pension plan ☐ Legal rep. ☐ 942 emp. ☐ Subtotal ☐ Deferred compensation ☐ Void ☐				
			7 Allocated tips		8 Advance EIC payment		
			9 Federal income tax withheld 1408.00		10 Wages, tips, other compensation 12480.00		
3 Employer's identification number 32-7654321		4 Employer's state I.D. number 095	11 Social security tax withheld 937.25		12 Social security wages 12480.00		
5 Employee's social security number 234-56-7890			13 Social security tips		14 Nonqualified plans		
19 Employee's name, address and ZIP code Robert J. Jackson 2357 Bluff Rd. North Spring, IL 68253			15 Dependent care benefits		16 Fringe benefits incl. in Box 10		
			17		18 Other		
20		21	22		23		
24 State income tax 287.00		25 State wages, tips, etc. 12480.00	26 Name of state IL	27 Local income tax	28 Local wages, tips, etc.		29 Name of locality

Copy B To be filed with employee's FEDERAL tax return Dept. of the Treasury—Internal Revenue Service

Form **W-2 Wage and Tax Statement 1990**

This information is being furnished to the Internal Revenue Service.

If 1040A, line 19, OR 1040EZ, line 5 is—		And you are—				If 1040A, line 19, OR 1040EZ, line 5 is—		And you are—				If 1040A, line 19, OR 1040EZ, line 5 is—		And you are—			
At least	But less than	Single (and 1040EZ filers)	Married filing jointly *	Married filing separately	Head of a household	At least	But less than	Single (and 1040EZ filers)	Married filing jointly *	Married filing separately	Head of a household	At least	But less than	Single (and 1040EZ filers)	Married filing jointly *	Married filing separately	Head of a household
		Your tax is—						Your tax is—						Your tax is—			
7,000						**10,000**						**13,000**					
7,000	7,050	1,054	1,054	1,054	1,054	10,000	10,050	1,504	1,504	1,504	1,504	13,000	13,050	1,954	1,954	1,954	1,954
7,050	7,100	1,061	1,061	1,061	1,061	10,050	10,100	1,511	1,511	1,511	1,511	13,050	13,100	1,961	1,961	1,961	1,961
7,100	7,150	1,069	1,069	1,069	1,069	10,100	10,150	1,519	1,519	1,519	1,519	13,100	13,150	1,969	1,969	1,969	1,969
7,150	7,200	1,076	1,076	1,076	1,076	10,150	10,200	1,526	1,526	1,526	1,526	13,150	13,200	1,976	1,976	1,976	1,976
7,200	7,250	1,084	1,084	1,084	1,084	10,200	10,250	1,534	1,534	1,534	1,534	13,200	13,250	1,984	1,984	1,984	1,984
7,250	7,300	1,091	1,091	1,091	1,091	10,250	10,300	1,541	1,541	1,541	1,541	13,250	13,300	1,991	1,991	1,991	1,991
7,300	7,350	1,099	1,099	1,099	1,099	10,300	10,350	1,549	1,549	1,549	1,549	13,300	13,350	1,999	1,999	1,999	1,999
7,350	7,400	1,106	1,106	1,106	1,106	10,350	10,400	1,556	1,556	1,556	1,556	13,350	13,400	2,006	2,006	2,006	2,006
7,400	7,450	1,114	1,114	1,114	1,114	10,400	10,450	1,564	1,564	1,564	1,564	13,400	13,450	2,014	2,014	2,014	2,014
7,450	7,500	1,121	1,121	1,121	1,121	10,450	10,500	1,571	1,571	1,571	1,571	13,450	13,500	2,021	2,021	2,021	2,021
7,500	7,550	1,129	1,129	1,129	1,129	10,500	10,550	1,579	1,579	1,579	1,579	13,500	13,550	2,029	2,029	2,029	2,029
7,550	7,600	1,136	1,136	1,136	1,136	10,550	10,600	1,586	1,586	1,586	1,586	13,550	13,600	2,036	2,036	2,036	2,036
7,600	7,650	1,144	1,144	1,144	1,144	10,600	10,650	1,594	1,594	1,594	1,594	13,600	13,650	2,044	2,044	2,044	2,044
7,650	7,700	1,151	1,151	1,151	1,151	10,650	10,700	1,601	1,601	1,601	1,601	13,650	13,700	2,051	2,051	2,051	2,051
7,700	7,750	1,159	1,159	1,159	1,159	10,700	10,750	1,609	1,609	1,609	1,609	13,700	13,750	2,059	2,059	2,059	2,059
7,750	7,800	1,166	1,166	1,166	1,166	10,750	10,800	1,616	1,616	1,616	1,616	13,750	13,800	2,066	2,066	2,066	2,066
7,800	7,850	1,174	1,174	1,174	1,174	10,800	10,850	1,624	1,624	1,624	1,624	13,800	13,850	2,074	2,074	2,074	2,074
7,850	7,900	1,181	1,181	1,181	1,181	10,850	10,900	1,631	1,631	1,631	1,631	13,850	13,900	2,081	2,081	2,081	2,081
7,900	7,950	1,189	1,189	1,189	1,189	10,900	10,950	1,639	1,639	1,639	1,639	13,900	13,950	2,089	2,089	2,089	2,089
7,950	8,000	1,196	1,196	1,196	1,196	10,950	11,000	1,646	1,646	1,646	1,646	13,950	14,000	2,096	2,096	2,096	2,096

(Continued)

Name _____

Form 1040EZ

Department of the Treasury - Internal Revenue Service

Income Tax Return for Single Filers With No Dependents (O) **19xx**

Name & address

Use the IRS mailing label. If you don't have one, please print.

LABEL HERE

Print your name above (first, initial, last)

Home address (number and street). (If you have a P.O. box, see back.) Apt. no.

City, town or post office, state, and ZIP code

Please print your numbers like this:

9 8 7 6 5 4 3 2 1 0

Your social security number

☐☐☐ ☐☐ ☐☐☐☐

Instructions are on the back. Also, see the Form 1040A/1040EZ booklet, especially the checklist on page 14.

Presidential Election Campaign Fund
Do you want $1 to go to this fund?

Note: Checking "Yes" will not change your tax or reduce your refund. ▶

Yes No
☐   ☐

Dollars Cents

Report your income

Attach Copy B of Form(s) W-2 here.

1 Total wages, salaries, and tips. This should be shown in Box 10 of your W-2 form(s). (Attach your W-2 form(s).) **1**

2 Taxable interest income of $400 or less. If the total is more than $400, you cannot use Form 1040EZ. **2**

3 Add line 1 and line 2. This is your **adjusted gross income**. **3**

Note: You must check Yes or No.

4 Can your parents (or someone else) claim you on their return?
☐ **Yes.** Do worksheet on back; enter amount from line E here.
☐ **No.** Enter 5,100. This is the total of your standard deduction and personal exemption. **4**

5 Subtract line 4 from line 3. If line 4 is larger than line 3, enter 0. This is your **taxable income**. **5**

Figure your tax

6 Enter your Federal income tax withheld from Box 9 of your W-2 form(s). **6**

7 **Tax.** Use the amount on **line 5** to look up your tax in the tax table on pages 41-46 of the Form 1040A/1040EZ booklet. Use the **single** column in the table. Enter the tax from the table on this line. **7**

Refund or amount you owe

Attach tax payment here.

8 If line 6 is larger than line 7, subtract line 7 from line 6. This is your **refund**. **8**

9 If line 7 is larger than line 6, subtract line 6 from line 7. This is the **amount you owe**. Attach check or money order for the full amount, payable to "Internal Revenue Service." **9**

Sign your return

(Keep a copy of this form for your records.)

I have read this return. Under penalties of perjury, I declare that to the best of my knowledge and belief, the return is true, correct, and complete.

Your signature _____ Date _____

X

For IRS Use Only—Please do not write in boxes below.

For Privacy Act and Paperwork Reduction Act Notice, see page 3 in the booklet. Form 1040EZ (19xx)

Paychecks and Taxes 99

READING A PAYCHECK STUB

Activity C
Chapter 19

Name _____
Date _____ Period _____

Use the paycheck stub shown below to answer the questions that follow.

1. What is Sarah's hourly wage? _____
2. How many hours did Sarah work last week? _____
3. What is Sarah's gross pay for this pay period? _____
4. How much was withheld from Sarah's gross pay for Federal income tax? _____
5. How much was withheld from Sarah's gross pay for Social Security tax? _____
6. What are Sarah's gross earnings so far this year? _____
7. How much state income tax has been withheld from Sarah's paycheck so far this year? _____
8. What is Sarah's net pay for this pay period? _____
9. If Sarah works 15 hours next week, what will her gross pay be? _____
10. What will Sarah's new year to date earnings total be after working 15 hours next week? _____

REGULAR RATE	REGULAR HOURS	OTHER HOURS	REGULAR EARNINGS	OTHER EARNINGS	TAXABLE ADJUSTMENT	NONTAXABLE ADJUSTMENT	TAXABLE GROSS EARNINGS
4.35	23.00		100.05				100.05

DEDUCTIONS

TOTAL EARNINGS	FED W/H TAX	FICA	STATE TAX	LOCAL TAX		
100.05	4.81	7.50	2.50			

YEAR TO DATE TOTALS

EARNINGS	FED W/H TAX	FICA	STATE TAX	LOCAL TAX		
1004.85	48.35	75.34	25.15			

OTHER DEDUCTIONS

INS.						

SOCIAL SECURITY NO.		CHECK NO.	PERIOD ENDING	NET PAY
123-45-6789	Sarah E. Goldberg	47503	3/16/xx	85.24

20 BUDGETS

REINFORCING VOCABULARY

Activity A
Chapter 20

Name _____

Date _____ Period _____

Write the correct term from the chapter in the blank before each statement. Then transfer your answers to the crossword puzzle.

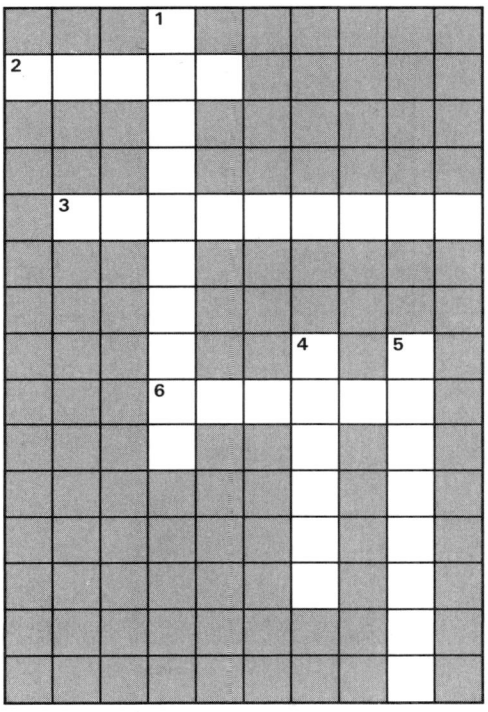

Across

_____ 2. A _____ expense involves a set amount of money due on a set date.

_____ 3. _____ expenses are paid four time a year.

_____ 6. _____ expenses are paid once a year.

Down

_____ 1. _____ expenses are paid twice a year.

_____ 4. A _____ is a plan for the use or management of money.

_____ 5. _____ expenses vary in amount.

Copyright Goodheart-Willcox Co., Inc.

Budgets 101

FIXED AND FLEXIBLE EXPENSES

Activity B Name _____

Chapter 20 Date _____ Period _____

Read the list of expenses below and decide whether each expense listed is fixed or flexible. List each expense under the appropriate column in the chart.

Movie tickets.

Rent payments.

Gasoline.

Jewelry.

New shoes.

Mortgage payments.

Makeup.

Automobile maintenance.

Amusement park tickets.

Telephone bills.

Loan payments.

Laundry.

Books and magazines.

Ice cream.

Auto insurance.

Automobile loan payments.

Birthday presents.

Savings.

Fixed Expenses	Flexible Expenses

MAKING YOUR MONEY WORK FOR YOU

Activity C Name _____

Chapter 20 Date _____ Period _____

Answer the following questions to help you evaluate your purchase goals before planning a budget.

1. What are your current sources of income? _____
   _____
   _____

2. Make a list of the three things you most want to buy now and in the future. List items you want within a year in the "now" column. List your long-range purchase goals in the "later" column. Use catalogs or newspaper ads to help you estimate the cost of each item on your list.

Now	Cost	Later	Cost
a. _____	$_____	_____	$_____
b. _____	$_____	_____	$_____
c. _____	$_____	_____	$_____
Total	$_____	Total	$_____

3. Will you be able to afford the items in your "now" column in a year or less? _____

   If so, what will be your next purchase goal? _____
   _____
   _____

   If not, how could you increase your income? _____
   _____
   _____

4. Are you currently saving any of your income? _____

   If so, what are your plans for the money you are saving? _____
   _____
   _____

   If not, how could you adjust your current spending pattern to start saving? _____
   _____
   _____

5. How could saving now help you reach some of the purchase goals in your "later" column? _____
   _____
   _____

PLANNING A BUDGET

Activity D   Name _____

Chapter 20   Date _____ Period _____

Complete this form to develop your own budget for one month. Include dollar amounts for the categories of spending that apply to you.

BUDGET PLANNING GUIDE

ESTIMATED INCOME
- Net income (wages) $ _____
- Tips   _____
- Other _____   _____
- TOTAL $ _____

ESTIMATED FIXED EXPENSES

Housing
- Rent or mortgage payments _____
- Maintenance fees _____
- Other _____ _____

Insurance Premiums
- Life _____
- Health/medical _____
- Automobile _____
- Home _____
- Other _____ _____

Debts and Obligations
- Automobile loan payments _____
- Other installment loan payments _____
- Contributions _____
- Tuition _____
- Membership dues _____
- Other _____ _____

Taxes and Licenses
- Property taxes _____
- Automobile license plates _____
- Other _____ _____

TOTAL $ _____

ESTIMATED FLEXIBLE EXPENSES

Food
- At home $ _____
- Away from home _____

Clothing and Accessories
- New clothes _____
- Cleaning and laundry _____
- Accessories _____
- Grooming aids _____

Household
- Home furnishings _____
- Maintenance and repair _____
- Gas _____
- Electricity _____
- Water _____
- Telephone _____

Transportation
- Gasoline _____
- Automobile maintenance _____
- Public transportation _____

Medical Needs
- Doctor _____
- Dentist _____
- Other _____ _____

Savings
- Savings account _____
- Bonds _____
- Other _____ _____

Recreation and Entertainment
- Movies _____
- Vacations _____
- Sport events _____
- Books and magazines _____
- Other _____ _____

TOTAL $ _____

SUMMARY

Total estimated income $ _____
Total estimated expenses
($ _____ fixed + $ _____ flexible)   − _____
BALANCE (income minus expenses) $ _____

If you have a positive balance (total estimated income is greater than total estimated expenses), what will you do with the extra money? _____

_____

If you have a negative balance (total estimated income is less than total estimated expenses), how will you adjust your income or expenses in order to have a workable budget? _____

_____

21 CHECKING ACCOUNTS

REINFORCING VOCABULARY

Activity A
Chapter 21

Name _____
Date _____ Period _____

Fill in the blanks with the chapter terms being described and then find them in the word maze. (Terms are located forward, backward, horizontally, and vertically in the maze.)

```
S C B T T Q H B N V K P L T E H K
K E J A N V V U T C C D I E K C C
C L S C H E C K B R E E B L R S E
E U A E U N M L L V H P T R N N H
H G C I O D S E O P C O R E P K C
C P R A W O S K T A D S R D S A S
S W A R D R E V O A E I D R A U R
R N T C B S A G C D I T F O D Q E
E F F O P E P H Y O F S O Y B B I
L A E X O M N C A J I L K E H T H
E H C S R E I H S A T I Q N G H S
V R J A T M Y Y A E R P D O A C A
A A N Z O T C S O T E H E M E B C
R S M I B U O I P R C K C E Z X V
T N E M E T A T S K N A B O E W M
```

_____ 1. A(n) _____ _____ is used to record how much money you put in your account.

_____ 2. A written order to pay someone is a(n) _____.

_____ 3. To _____ a check is to sign your name on the back of a check made out to you so you can cash it.

_____ 4. When you _____ your account, you write checks for more money than you have.

_____ 5. The _____ _____ lists all of your deposits, withdrawals (in the form of checks), service charges, and interest payments.

_____ 6. When you pay by _____ _____, the bank withdraws the requested amount from your checking account and guarantees payment.

_____ 7. A(n) _____ _____ is drawn by the bank on its own funds.

_____ 8. A(n) _____ _____ is an order to pay a certain amount of money to a certain party and can be purchased from several places.

_____ 9. _____ _____ are purchased to avoid taking cash on vacation.

USING A CHECKING ACCOUNT

Activity B
Chapter 21

Name _____

Date _____ Period _____

Using the information below, practice writing checks, completing a deposit slip, and filling in a check register. The checks are all to be written in October of the current year. Fill in your own name and address in the blanks at the top of each check and the deposit slip. Your beginning balance is $150.10.

Check Number	Date	Transaction	
102	10/5	Shop Rite (groceries)	$ 50.00
103	10/11	Sears (charge account #23596)	$ 44.20
104	10/20	Easly Life Insurance Co.	$ 36.50
	10/21	Deposit (Check 16-214)	$ 250.00

(Continued)

Name _____

	No. 104
	_____ 19 ____ 00-6789/0000

Pay to the order of _____ $ _____

_____ DOLLARS

FINANCIAL INSTITUTION
YOUR CITY, U.S.A. 12345

SAMPLE-VOID
DELUXE CHECK PRINTERS, INCORPORATED

Memo _____

⑆000067894⑆ 12345678⑊

DEPOSIT

NAME _____

DATE _____ 19 ____

FINANCIAL INSTITUTION
YOUR CITY, U.S.A. 12345

⑆000067894⑆ 12345678⑊

DELUXE SDT-3 (NAK)   ALL ITEMS ARE ACCEPTED SUBJECT TO OUR RULES AND REGULATIONS APPLICABLE TO THIS ACCOUNT.

CASH	CURRENCY		
	COIN		
C H E C K S			
TOTAL FROM OTHER SIDE			
➤	TOTAL		
	LESS CASH RECEIVED		
	NET DEPOSIT		

00-6789/0000

USE OTHER SIDE FOR ADDITIONAL LISTING

BE SURE EACH ITEM IS PROPERLY ENDORSED

RECORD ALL CHARGES OR CREDITS THAT AFFECT YOUR ACCOUNT

NUMBER	DATE	DESCRIPTION OF TRANSACTION	PAYMENT/DEBIT (−)	√T	FEE (IF ANY) (−)	DEPOSIT/CREDIT (+)	BALANCE $
			$		$	$	

REMEMBER TO RECORD AUTOMATIC PAYMENTS / DEPOSITS ON DATE AUTHORIZED.

Copyright Goodheart-Willcox Co., Inc. Checking Accounts

BALANCING A CHECKBOOK

Activity C   Name _____

Chapter 21   Date _____ Period _____

Use the bank statement and check register that follow to help Peter Banks balance his checking account.

TWIN CITY BANK
Toms River, NJ 58625

ACCOUNT NUMBER
555-1212
PAGE 1
NO. OF CHECKS 4

THIS STATEMENT DATE AND BALANCE	DEBITS AMOUNT	NUMBER	SERVICE CHARGE
1/28/9x 210.85	61.75	4	2.50

LAST STATEMENT DATE AND BALANCE	CREDITS AMOUNT	NUMBER	INTEREST
12/28/9x 125.10	150.00	2	0.00

STATEMENT OF ACCOUNT

Peter Banks
222 Atlantic Avenue
Toms River, NJ 58625

DAY	REF	CHECKS AND OTHER DEBITS	AMT	REF	CHECKS AND OTHER DEBITS	AMT	DEPOSITS AND OTHER CREDITS	DAILY BALANCE
1-8	501		11.75					113.35
1-9	502		15.00					98.35
1-10	DEPOSIT						85.00	183.35
1-17	DEPOSIT						65.00	248.35
1-21	504		20.00					228.35
1-22	503		15.00					213.35
1-28			2.50		SERVICE CHARGE			210.85

(Continued)

Name _____

● Use the check (✓) column on the register to check off items that appear on the bank statement. Remember to add interest shown on the statement to Peter's checkbook balance. Remember to subtract service charges shown on the statement from his balance.

NUMBER	DATE	DESCRIPTION OF TRANSACTION	PAYMENT/DEBIT (−)	✓T	FEE (IF ANY) (−)	DEPOSIT/CREDIT (+)	BALANCE $125 10	
501	1/5	Telephone Company (December phone bill)	$ 11 75	$	$		11 113	75 35
502	1/6	Cash	15 00				15 98	00 35
	1/10	Deposit				85 00	85 183	00 35
503	1/16	J.J. Garage (Oil and lube)	15 00				15 168	00 35
504	1/16	Green Thumb Florist (Flower Arrangement)	20 00				20 148	00 35
	1/17	Deposit				65 00	65 213	00 35
505	1/20	Pleasant Hill Apartment (February rent)	195 00				195 18	00 35
	1/29	Deposit				210 00	210 228	00 35

Complete this form to make sure Peter's checkbook balances against his bank statement.

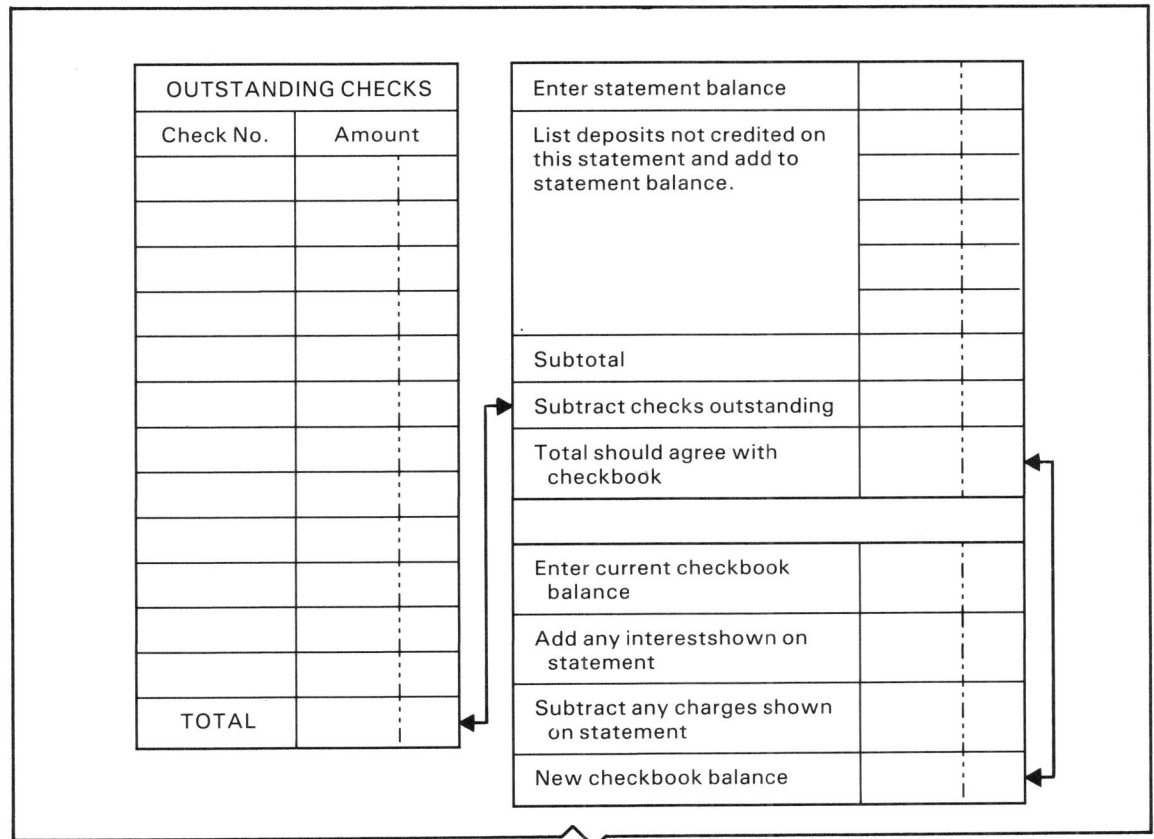

CORRECTING AN IMBALANCE

Activity D
Chapter 21

Name _____
Date _____ Period _____

Karen's checkbook register does not balance against her bank statement. Check to make sure that Karen did not make any math errors in her register. Write the numbers that should appear in the balance column in the spaces provided beside the checkbook register. Then answer the questions at the bottom of the page.

NUMBER	DATE	DESCRIPTION OF TRANSACTION	PAYMENT/DEBIT (-)	√T	FEE (IF ANY) (-)	DEPOSIT/CREDIT (+)	BALANCE
							$335.00
206	2/3	Central Bank (Car Payment)	$135.00				135.00
							200.00
207	2/7	Cindy Wright (birthday present)	15.00				15.00
							185.00
	2/7	Deposit				315.65	315.65
							500.65
208	2/9	City Utilities (January bill)	33.69				33.69
							476.06
209	2/11	Midwest Bell (Telephone bill)	22.10				22.10
							453.96
211	2/19	Exclusive Clothier (party dress)	78.83				78.83
							375.13
	2/21	Deposit				275.00	275.00
							650.13
212	2/28	Skyview Apartments (March rent)	295.00				295.00
							355.13

1. _____
2. _____
3. _____
4. _____
5. _____
6. _____
7. _____
8. _____

DAY	REF	CHECKS AND OTHER DEBITS	AMT	REF	CHECKS AND OTHER DEBITS	AMT	DEPOSITS AND OTHER CREDITS	DAILY BALANCE
2-06	206		135.00					200.00
2-07	DEPOSIT						315.65	515.65
2-11	207		15.00					500.65
2-14	209		22.10					478.55
2-15	208		33.69					444.86
2-17	210		59.70					385.16
2-21	DEPOSIT						275.00	660.16
2-23	211		78.83					581.33
3-03	212		295.00					286.33
3-05			4.00		SERVICE CHARGE			282.33

9. Besides math errors, what other mistakes did Karen make? _____

_____

10. Correct the mistakes you listed in question 9. What should the balance in Karen's register now read?

_____

SAVINGS

REINFORCING VOCABULARY

Activity A
Chapter 22

Name _____
Date _____ Period _____

Complete the sentences by writing the correct chapter terms from the list below in the blanks provided.

Certificates of deposit
Commercial banks
Compound interest
Credit unions
Interest

Passbook savings account
Principal
Savings and loan
Savings club
U.S. savings bonds

_____ 1. _____ _____ are financial institutions that offer a full variety of banking services.

_____ 2. _____ _____ _____ associations are financial institutions that are known for loaning money to home buyers.

_____ 3. Nonprofit financial institutions owned by and operated for their members are called _____ _____.

_____ 4. When you open a _____ _____ _____, you receive a small book in which your deposits and withdrawals will be recorded.

_____ 5. Money paid to you for allowing a financial institution to use your money is known as _____.

_____ 6. The _____ is the amount of your original deposit in an account.

_____ 7. Interest that is earned on both the principal and the earned interest is _____ _____.

_____ 8. An account in which you deposit a set amount of money every week or month is called a(n) _____ _____.

_____ 9. _____ _____ _____ are purchased for a certain amount of money and are held for a set period of time.

_____ 10. _____ _____ _____ are certificates of debt issued by the federal government.

SAVINGS SURVEY

Activity B Name _____

Chapter 22 Date _____ Period _____

If you have a savings account, answer the following questions based on your savings experience. If you do not have a savings account, use these questions to interview someone who does. Compare your answers with others in class.

1. Is saving money important to you? Explain why or why not. _____
_____
_____

2. Rank the following reasons for saving from 1 (most important) to 7 (least important) in order of their importance to you.
   _____ Emergencies.
   _____ Loss of income.
   _____ Travel and recreation.
   _____ Advanced education.
   _____ Major purchases, such as a car or home.
   _____ Retirement.
   _____ Overall financial security.

3. Aside from the reasons listed above, what other reasons do you have for saving money? _____
_____

4. What advantages do you feel there are to saving money through a financial institution over saving money at home? _____
_____
_____

5. What type of savings account do you have? _____
6. In what type of financial institution is your savings account? _____
7. What interest rate does your savings account earn? _____
8. How often is interest paid on your savings? _____
9. How often do you make deposits into your savings? _____
10. How often do you withdraw money from your savings? _____
11. Do you have more than one savings account? If so, how many accounts do you have? _____
12. Describe your other account(s) in terms of the information included in questions 5 through 10.
_____
_____
_____

13. Besides a savings account, what other financial services does your financial institution offer that you have used? _____
_____

14. What advice would you give to someone who was thinking about opening a savings account?
_____
_____

FINANCIAL INSTITUTIONS

Activity C Name _____

Chapter 22 Date _____ Period _____

Obtain brochures describing a local bank, savings and loan, and credit union and the services they offer. Complete the chart with what you learn about each financial institution. Then answer the questions that follow.

BANK	SAVINGS AND LOAN	CREDIT UNION
Name:	Name:	Name:
Location:	Location:	Location:
	Hours:	Hours:
Interest on savings accounts:	Interest on savings accounts:	Interest on savings accounts:
Services offered:	Services offered:	Services offered:

In what ways are these financial institutions similar? _____

_____

_____

In what ways are these financial institutions different? _____

_____

_____

If you were opening a new savings account, which one of these institutions would you choose? Explain your answer. _____

_____

_____

SAVINGS DEPOSITS AND WITHDRAWALS

Activity D   Name _____

Chapter 22   Date _____ Period _____

Complete the deposit slip and withdrawal slip below. Use your name, today's date, and the other information provided.

Deposit slip: You want to deposit the following:
3 twenties, 1 ten, and 3 ones in currency.
160 quarters, 100 dimes, 40 nickels, and 300 pennies in coins.
check 14-610 for $32.10 and check 70-7211 for $43.83.
You want to receive a $50 bill.

SAVINGS DEPOSIT

ACCOUNT NO. _____

NAME _____

DATE _____ 19 ____

_____

FINANCIAL INSTITUTION
YOUR CITY, U.S.A. 12345

CASH	CURRENCY		
	COIN		
CHECKS			
TOTAL FROM OTHER SIDE			
TOTAL			
LESS CASH RECEIVED			
NET DEPOSIT			

00-6789/0000

USE OTHER SIDE FOR ADDITIONAL LISTING

BE SURE EACH ITEM IS PROPERLY ENDORSED

ALL ITEMS ARE ACCEPTED SUBJECT TO OUR RULES AND REGULATIONS APPLICABLE TO THIS ACCOUNT.

Withdrawal slip: You want to withdraw $40.00 from your account.

SAVINGS WITHDRAWAL must be presented by the savings customer in person or by mail.

NAME _____ ACCOUNT NO. _____
PLEASE TYPE OR PRINT CLEARLY

_____ 19 ____   00-6789/0000

_____ Dollars $ _____

DEDUCT ABOVE SUM FROM MY SAVINGS ACCOUNT
ON DEPOSIT WITH:

FINANCIAL INSTITUTION
YOUR CITY, U.S.A. 12345   SIGN HERE _____

CREDIT

REINFORCING VOCABULARY

Activity A
Chapter 23

Name _____

Date _____ Period _____

Write the correct term from the chapter in the blank before each statement. Then transfer your answers to the crossword puzzle.

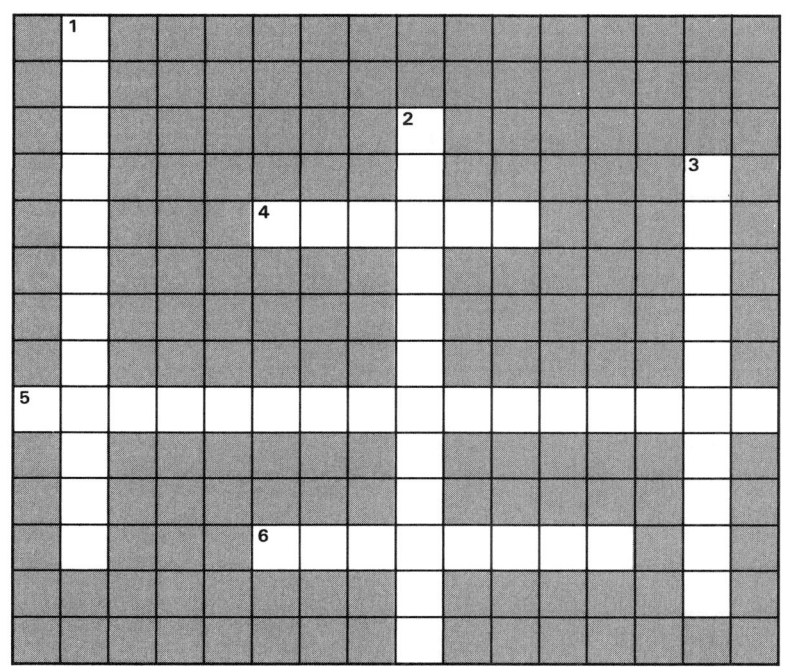

Across

_____ 4. Valuable possessions you own, money you have in bank accounts, and the value of stocks and bonds you own are examples of _____.

_____ 5. Contracts that legally bind a lender and a borrower to credit terms described in writing are called _____ _____.

_____ 6. A(n) _____ is someone who guarantees that your loan will be paid and must make the payments if you do not.

Down

_____ 1. The _____ _____ checks credit applications and gathers financial information on people to help businesses decide whether to grant or deny people credit.

_____ 2. An estimate of how likely you are to repay your bills on time is your _____ _____.

_____ 3. _____ is something of value held by a lending institution in case you fail to repay.

CREDIT ADVANTAGES AND DISADVANTAGES

Activity B   Name _____

Chapter 23   Date _____ Period_____

Read each statement and place an "A" in the blank if it is an advantage of using credit and a "D" in the blank if it is a disadvantage of using credit. Then respond to the requests below.

_____ 1. Credit is a convenience.

_____ 2. Credit encourages impulse buying.

_____ 3. Credit allows you to use goods and services while paying for them.

_____ 4. Credit helps you meet financial emergencies.

_____ 5. Credit ties up your future income.

_____ 6. Credit makes the costs of goods and services higher.

_____ 7. Credit can get you into serious debt.

_____ 8. Credit can cause you to overspend.

_____ 9. Credit allows you to shop and travel without the worry of carrying large amounts of cash.

_____ 10. Credit helps you buy expensive items and pay for them over a period of time.

Describe a real or fictitious situation in which a person uses the advantages of credit to benefit him or her.

_____

_____

_____

_____

Describe a real or fictitious situation in which a person abuses credit and the disadvantages of credit cause him or her harm. _____

_____

_____

_____

When would you use credit?_____

_____

_____

When would you avoid using credit? _____

_____

_____

THE COST OF CREDIT

Activity C Name _____

Chapter 23 Date _____ Period _____

Complete the following exercises to figure the cost of using various types of credit.

Credit card. Your credit card balance for this month is $60. You can pay the balance in full, or you can make a minimum payment of $10 each month. If you choose to make the minimum payment, you will be charged 1.5 percent interest per month (18 percent annual interest) on the unpaid balance. The steps below use the first month as an example to show you how to figure the cost of carrying an unpaid balance.

Step 1: Subtract the minimum payment from the total balance.
$60.00 − 10.00 = $50.00

Step 2: Multiply the answer to step one by the interest rate (.015). This is the cost of delaying full payment for another month.
$50.00 × .015 = $ .75

Step 3: Add the answers to steps one and two. This figure is the new balance that will appear on next month's bill. Use this figure as the new total balance in step one.
$50.00 + .75 = $50.75

Figure the total cost of making minimum payments until the bill is paid off by repeating the above steps.

Month 2:
Step 1: $50.75 − 10.00 = $_____
Step 2: $_____ × .015 = $_____
Step 3: $_____ + _____ = $_____

Month 3:
Step 1: $_____ − 10.00 = $_____
Step 2: $_____ × .015 = $_____
Step 3: $_____ + _____ = $_____

Month 4:
Step 1: $_____ − 10.00 = $_____
Step 2: $_____ × .015 = $_____
Step 3: $_____ + _____ = $_____

Month 5:
Step 1: $_____ − 10.00 = $_____
Step 2: $_____ × .015 = $_____
Step 3: $_____ + _____ = $_____

Month 6:
Pay remaining balance in full at this time. Add together the six monthly payments. Then subtract the original total balance from this sum. What was the total cost of delaying full payment on this credit card bill?

_____

Installment credit. The cash price of a television is $600.00. However, you can purchase the television on credit by paying $100.00 cash now and $46.67 each month for the next 12 months.

Step 1: Multiply the amount of each payment by the number of payments.
$_____ × _____ = $_____

Step 2: Add the cash payment to the answer in step 1. This is the total cost of the television.
$_____ + _____ = $_____

Step 3: Subtract the cash price from the answer to step 2. This is the cost of using credit.
$_____ − _____ = $_____

Credit 117

THE CREDIT GAME

Activity D Name _____

Chapter 23 Date _____ Period _____

Evaluate your credit history as you play the game below. Use buttons, circles of paper, or coins for markers and flip a coin to move around the board. If the coin is flipped "heads," move the marker two spaces. If the coin is flipped "tails," move the marker one space. The player who finishes first is the winner.

1. START	2. Your savings account shows a steady pattern of saving over the last three years. Move ahead 1 space.	3.	4. Your charge accounts with the local gas and electric companies show that you frequently pay late fees. Move back 1 space.
8.	7. You are already spending 20 percent of your take-home pay on installment debts. You cannot afford any more credit. Go back to start.	6.	5. You just got a job! Your steady source of income makes you a good credit risk. Take another turn.
9. You pay the total due on your gasoline credit card on time each month. Move ahead 2 spaces.	18. Easy credit has caused you to fall into a pattern of impulse buying. Miss a turn to give yourself time to plan your next purchases.	17.	16. You've gotten a reputation for making layaway payments on time at a local department store. Move ahead 1 space.
10. Your credit cards are always charged to the limit and you've carried a large unpaid balance for the last 15 months. Miss a turn while you pay off some of your debt.	19.	20. **FINISH** Congratulations! You've shown that you can manage money responsibly and use credit wisely.	15. Your loan fell through because the credit bureau said that your cosigner has a worse credit history than you do. Move back to space 10.
11.	12. You purchased a new TV on installment credit. You failed to make your payments and the set was repossessed. Move back 1 space.	13. You've repaid a loan to your company credit union in a timely fashion. Take another turn.	14. BUY NOW PAY LATER!

24 INSURANCE

REINFORCING VOCABULARY

Activity A
Chapter 24

Name _____
Date _____ Period _____

Match the following chapter terms and definitions. Then write a paragraph using the chapter terms to describe a fictitious person's insurance situation.

_____ 1. Legal contract that describes your rights and responsibilities and the rights and responsibilities of the insurance company.

_____ 2. The amount of money you pay for insurance.

_____ 3. The amount of money you must pay before the insurance company begins paying on a claim.

_____ 4. Type of health insurance in which set fees that cover most health care services are paid in advance.

_____ 5. Permanent life insurance that is in effect until the insured dies or the policy is cashed in.

_____ 6. Life insurance purchased for a limited period of time.

a. Deductible.
b. Health maintenance organization (HMO).
c. Policy.
d. Premium.
e. Term life insurance.
f. Whole life insurance.

UNDERSTANDING INSURANCE

Activity B
Chapter 24

Name _____

Date _____ Period _____

Answer the following questions to show your understanding of the concepts presented in the chapter.

1. What is the difference between the insurer and the insured? _____

2. What type of automobile insurance protects you against the claims of other people? _____

3. What type of automobile insurance protects you against court actions or claims for injuries to other people? _____

4. What type of automobile insurance protects other people's property against damage that you cause? _____

5. What type of automobile insurance pays for repairs to your car even if you are at fault? _____

6. Why might a person decide not to carry collision insurance on his or her automobile? _____

7. Name three costs besides hospital stays and examinations by physicians that may be covered under health insurance. _____

8. What is an advantage of having group health insurance rather than buying health insurance on your own? _____

9. What is a beneficiary? _____

10. What is cash value? _____

11. What is an advantage of term life insurance over whole life insurance? _____

12. Compared with a married person, does a single person need more or less life insurance? _____

13. Who receives benefits under disability insurance? _____

14. What is the purpose of property insurance? _____

15. What type of property insurance pays the full cost of new items? _____

16. How can a personal property inventory be helpful to a renter or homeowner? _____

17. Give an example of a situation in which you would need to file a claim. _____

Copyright Goodheart-Willcox Co., Inc.

CAR INSURANCE COSTS

Activity C Name _____

Chapter 24 Date _____ Period_____

Contact a local insurance company. Request the necessary information to complete the form below regarding automobile insurance coverage. Then choose the types of coverage you would like to have and figure your total premium. Compare your form with classmates to see if another company would offer you lower rates.

Company _____

1. What are the premium costs for the following types of coverage?

    a. Bodily injury insurance _____

    What is the limit of liability per person? _____ per accident? _____

    b. Property damage insurance _____

    What is the limit of liability per accident? _____

    c. Collision insurance _____

    What deductibles are available? _____

2. What other types of auto coverage are available and what is the cost for each type?

    a. _____

    b. _____

    c. _____

3. What discounts are available and what is the value of each discount?

    a. _____

    b. _____

    c. _____

List the types of automobile coverage offered by this company you would like to have and the cost for each type.

Coverage	Cost
a. _____	_____
b. _____	_____
c. _____	_____
d. _____	_____
e. _____	_____
Total	_____

List the discounts for which you would qualify and the value of each discount.

Discount	Value
a. _____	_____
b. _____	_____
Total	_____

Subtract the total value of the discounts from the total cost of the insurance. What is your total premium? _____

Insurance 121

PERSONAL PROPERTY INVENTORY

Activity D Name _____

Chapter 24 Date _____ Period_____

Keeping a current record of your property will help you in reporting lost or stolen property. Use this form to take inventory of your property.

ITEM DESCRIPTION (Include model #, serial #, or brand name name when possible	DATE OF PURCHASE	PURCHASE PRICE + TAX	PLACE OF PURCHASE

25 A PLACE TO LIVE

REINFORCING VOCABULARY

Activity A
Chapter 25

Name _____

Date _____ Period _____

Fill in the blanks with the correct chapter terms.

    Furnished apartment   Roommate
    Lease   Security deposit
    Real estate   Unfurnished apartment
    Rental agency   Verbal agreement

_____ 1. Flea markets and garage sales are good places to shop for low-cost items needed in a(n) _____ _____.

_____ 2. An apartment owner will use a tenant's _____ _____ to make necessary repairs due to damage caused by the tenant.

_____ 3. A(n) _____ explains in writing the rights and responsibilities of the tenant and the owner.

_____ 4. Living with a(n) _____ is an alternative to living at home or living alone.

_____ 5. A(n) _____ _____ will refer a person to available apartments for a fee.

_____ 6. A tenant renting a(n) _____ _____ may not need to supply any furniture of his or her own.

_____ 7. When a tenant and an owner agree on a rental arrangement without putting anything in writing, they make a(n) _____ _____.

_____ 8. Although most _____ _____ agencies handle the buying and selling of houses, some also handle rental properties.

APARTMENT SEARCH

Activity B   Name _____

Chapter 25   Date _____ Period _____

Using the classified section of the newspaper, gather information about one furnished and two unfurnished apartments to complete the chart below. Then answer the questions that follow.

	Furnished Apartment	Unfurnished Apartment A	Unfurnished Apartment B
Address			
Number of bedrooms			
Monthly rent			
What utilities are included in the rent?			
Security deposit required			
Length of lease			
Amount of storage space			
Is on-site parking available?			
Is it near public transportation?			
Are on-site laundry facilities available?			

Which of the three apartments you investigated would you most like to rent? Explain your answer.
_____
_____

Which of the three apartments you investigated would you least like to rent? Explain your answer. _____
_____
_____

Would you rather rent a furnished or an unfurnished apartment? Explain your answer. _____
_____
_____

Would you rather live alone or share an apartment with a roommate? Explain your answer. _____
_____
_____

FURNISHING AN APARTMENT

Activity C   Name _____

Chapter 25   Date _____ Period _____

In the chart below, list all the furnishings you would need if you moved into an unfurnished apartment. Don't forget to include items such as linens, dishes, cookware, and cleaning supplies in addition to furniture. For each item listed, check the appropriate column to indicate whether you would borrow it (or receive it as a gift), buy it used, or buy it new. Use the classified ads in your newspaper to estimate prices of the "used" items you plan to buy. Use store ads or catalogs to estimate prices of the "new" items you plan to buy. Then add the total of your planned purchases.

Item	Borrow/ Gift	Buy Used	Buy New	Estimated Price
			TOTAL	

HOUSING COSTS

Activity D   Name _____

Chapter 25   Date _____ Period _____

Complete this activity to help you estimate the cost of moving into an apartment.

1. Assume you were to rent one of the unfurnished apartments you investigated in Activity B. What is your monthly rent? _____

2. For any utilities not included in the rent, ask the owner of the apartment or your local utility companies what a typical monthly bill would be. Enter all expenses that would apply to you.

   Electric company monthly bill   _____

   Gas company monthly bill   _____

   Water company monthly bill   _____

   Telephone company monthly bill   _____

   Total   _____

3. Add the totals from items 1 and 2.
   _____ + _____ = _____

4. Some guidelines suggest limiting your rent and utility costs to one-third of your take-home pay. Using this guideline, what would your take-home pay need to be if you were living in this apartment? _____

5. Some additional expenses occur when you first move into an apartment. Contact the apartment owner and your local utility companies to enter all expenses that would apply to you.

   Credit check by apartment owner   _____

   Security deposit for apartment   _____

   Electric company deposit   _____

   Gas company deposit   _____

   Water company deposit   _____

   Telephone company deposit   _____

   Furnishings (from Activity C)   _____

   Total   _____

6. List other items you would need to pay for if you were living in an apartment (food, laundry, transportation or gasoline, insurance, etc.). _____
   _____
   _____

7. After having completed the above, what have you determined about the cost of independent living?
   _____
   _____

8. What could you do to reduce some of your expenses? _____
   _____
   _____

26 TRANSPORTATION

REINFORCING VOCABULARY

Activity A　　　　　　　　　　　　Name _____

Chapter 26　　　　　　　　　　　　Date _____ Period _____

Match the following chapter terms and definitions.

_____ 1. A list of the expected arrival and departure times and locations for buses, trains, subways, and airplanes.

_____ 2. A group of people who take turns driving to a common location or area.

_____ 3. Transportation, such as buses or trains, used by a large number of people.

_____ 4. To change from one bus or train route to another in order to get to the right place.

_____ 5. An organization that operates a transportation system.

a. Car pool.
b. Carrier.
c. Mass transportation.
d. Schedule.
e. Transfer.

In the space below, write a one- or two-paragraph story about someone who is traveling to work. Correctly use all of the chapter terms listed in the right column above.

_____
_____
_____
_____
_____
_____
_____
_____
_____
_____
_____
_____
_____
_____
_____
_____
_____
_____

READING A BUS SCHEDULE

Activity B   Name _____

Chapter 26   Date _____ Period _____

Use the bus schedule on the next page to answer the questions below.

1. What telephone number would you use to find out what time you could catch a bus at the Broad Street stop? _____

2. What telephone number would you use to complain about a rude bus driver? _____

3. On what holidays does this schedule operate? _____
   _____

4. On what days of the week does this schedule not operate? _____
   _____

5. What five activities are prohibitied on the bus? _____
   _____

6. Can passengers expect to get change from the bus driver? Explain why or why not. _____
   _____

7. Approximately how many minutes is the ride from Green Street to Spring Road? _____

8. On what bus line is the Park Avenue stop? _____

9. What does the O symbol mean? _____

10. Suppose you arrive at Industry Park at 5:50 P.M. on the Downtown Express. How long will you have to wait at the stop for a North Loop bus to arrive? _____

11. Which bus lines stop at Capitol Towers? _____

12. What time does the first Downtown Express bus arrive at Industry Park? _____

13. What time does the last bus of the day arrive at Glenwood Plaza, and which bus line is it? ____
    _____

14. How would you get from Carson Parkway to Glenwood Plaza? _____
    _____

15. Suppose you lived near the Center Street stop and had an appointment on Oak Street at 9:30 A.M. Which buses on which lines would you use to get there? _____
    _____
    _____

16. Name all the stops on the Center/Arbor line. _____
    _____
    _____

RAPID Bus Weekday Rush

	North Loop Line originates Columbus Blvd. 7:20 A.M.	Downtown Express originates Highland Rd. 7:45 A.M.	Center/Arbor Line originates Center St. 7:30 A.M.
Industry Park	7:55 A.M. 8:25 A.M. 8:55 A.M. 4:55 P.M. 5:25 P.M. 5:55 P.M.	7:50 A.M. 8:20 A.M. 8:50 A.M. 4:50 P.M. 5:20 P.M. 5:50 P.M.	———
Fountain Square	7:35 A.M. 8:05 A.M. 8:35 A.M. 4:35 P.M. 5:05 P.M. 5:35 P.M.	———	7:45 A.M. 8:45 A.M. 9:45 A.M. 6:15 P.M. 7:15 P.M. 8:15 P.M.
Capitol Towers	7:40 A.M. 8:10 A.M. 8:40 A.M. 4:40 P.M. 5:10 P.M. 5:40 P.M.	8:10 A.M. 8:40 A.M. 9:10 A.M. 5:10 P.M. 5:40 P.M. 6:10 P.M.	———
Glenwood Plaza	———	8:15 A.M. 8:45 A.M. 9:15 A.M. 5:15 P.M. 5:45 P.M. 6:15 P.M.	7:55 A.M. 8:55 A.M. 9:55 A.M. 6:25 P.M. 7:25 P.M. 8:25 P.M.

This schedule operates Monday through Friday, including Presidents' Day, Columbus Day, and Veterans' Day.

This schedule does not operate Saturdays, Sundays, or the following holidays: New Year's Day, Memorial Day, Independence Day, Labor Day, Thanksgiving, and Christmas.

For schedule information, call 555-TRIP.
For customer service, call 555-HELP.

Passengers must have exact fare. No eating, drinking, smoking, littering, or loud radio playing allowed on RAPID buses.

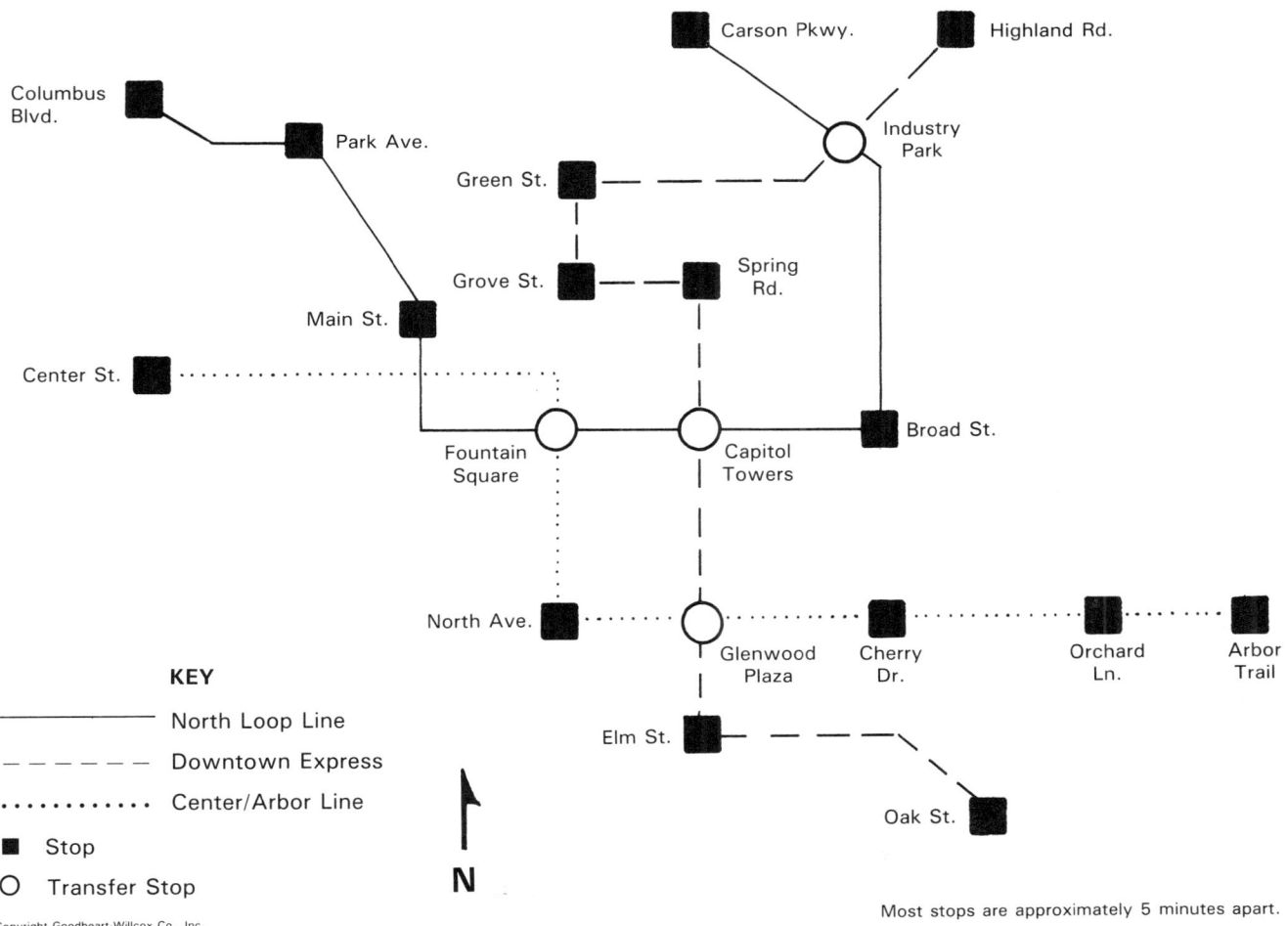

KEY
——— North Loop Line
- - - - - Downtown Express
.... Center/Arbor Line
■ Stop
○ Transfer Stop

Copyright Goodheart-Willcox Co., Inc.

Most stops are approximately 5 minutes apart.

TRANSPORTATION COMPARISON

Activity C   Name _____

Chapter 26   Date _____ Period _____

Complete the chart to indicate what you consider to be the advantages and disadvantages of using various types of transportation. Then answer the questions that follow.

	ADVANTAGES	DISADVANTAGES
Self-powered transportation Walking		
Riding a bicycle		
Automobile transportation Drive yourself		
Car pool		
Mass transportation Buses		
Trains and subways		
Airplanes		

1. Which type of transportation would you be most likely to use to get to work? Explain your answer.
_____

   Under what circumstances might you choose another type of transportation?
_____
_____

2. Which type of transportation would you be least likely to use to get to work? Explain your answer.
_____
_____

   Under what circumstances would you use this type of transportation? _____
_____

27 BEING A RESPONSIBLE CITIZEN

REINFORCING VOCABULARY

Activity A
Chapter 27

Name _____
Date _____ Period _____

Across
4. To make a new state law, a legislator introduces a _____ to the members of the legislature.
5. A company with a _____ has exclusive possession and control of a product or service.
6. When you _____, you add your name to the official list of citizens eligible to vote in elections.
7. A person who owes allegiance to a government is a _____.

Down
1. _____ laws define a person's rights in relation to government.
2. A public question appearing on a voting ballot for the consideration of voters is called a _____.
3. _____ laws relate to cases involving such issues as contracts, inheritances, and the business of corporations.

Being a Responsible Citizen 131

CITIZEN AWARENESS

Activity B
Chapter 27

Name _____

Date _____ Period _____

Read the following statements about topics from the chapter. Circle T if the statement is true. Circle F is the statement is false.

T F 1. Any citizen of the United States who is at least 21 years old has the right to vote.

T F 2. Citizens are responsible for making laws.

T F 3. In order to vote, a citizen must register.

T F 4. Citizens can register to vote at most lawyers' offices.

T F 5. Federal laws are made by the United States Congress.

T F 6. A debate is the discussion of a proposed law by members of the legislature.

T F 7. Citizens may vote to accept a proposition, causing it to become a law.

T F 8. Local bills may be printed in the newspaper before being brought to a vote at town council meetings.

T F 9. The laws in the United States are divided into two categories: criminal laws and international laws.

T F 10. Civil laws relate to cases involving such issues as contracts, inheritances, and the business of corporations.

T F 11. Presidents, governors, and mayors are members of the executive branches of federal, state, and local governments, respectively.

T F 12. Most lawyers handle all types of cases, so any lawyer could deal with any legal problems a person might have.

T F 13. A person who is unable to afford a lawyer has no way to receive help with a legal problem.

T F 14. The only time a person needs a lawyer is if he or she is arrested.

T F 15. Citizens participate in the economy by producing and consuming goods and services.

T F 16. Manufacturers can make any claims they wish on the labels of their products, whether or not they are true.

T F 17. Monopolies are against the law.

T F 18. Consumers have a responsibility to report products that they find to be unsafe.

T F 19. Many stores will not give refunds for returned items that were purchased on sale.

T F 20. Writing letters to the Better Business Bureau is the first step in correcting consumer problems.

VOTERS' SURVEY

Activity C
Chapter 27

Name _____

Date _____ Period _____

Survey five adults about their voting habits and opinions. Record their responses in the chart provided. Compile your results with those of your classmates. Write an article for your school or local newspaper reporting your findings.

1. What is your sex? a. Male. b. Female.

2. What is your age? a. 18 to 25. b. 26 to 40. c. 41 to 65. d. Over 65.

3. Are you registered to vote? a. Yes. b. No.

4. How often do you vote?
    a. In most national, state, and local elections.
    b. Only in national elections.
    c. Never.

5. How important do you feel it is for citizens to exercise their right to vote?
    a. Very important.
    b. Somewhat important.
    c. Somewhat unimportant.
    d. Not at all important.

6. What do you think is the most common reason why some citizens do not vote?
    a. They are not familiar with the candidates and/or issues.
    b. They do not care about the results of the election.
    c. They do not feel their individual votes make a difference.
    d. They are too busy.
    e. Other. (Write the reason given in the chart.)

7. Do you now the names of your elected officials? a. Yes. b. No.

8. Do you feel you understand how laws are made? a. Yes. b. No.

SURVEY RESPONSES

QUESTION	PERSON 1	PERSON 2	PERSON 3	PERSON 4	PERSON 5
1.					
2.					
3.					
4.					
5.					
6.					
7.					
8.					

Being a Responsible Citizen

CLASSROOM COUNCIL

Activity D   **Name** _____

Chapter 27   **Date** _____ **Period** _____

Hold a classroom election to elect seven students to serve as members of a classroom council—the governing body of your classroom. Complete the items below to pass a law in your classroom.

1. Write a law that you would like to propose to the citizens of your classroom. Be sure to choose the wording of your bill carefully. Citizens may not vote for bills that are not clear and specific.
   _____
   _____

2. List the reasons you would give for having the law.
   a. _____
   b. _____
   c. _____

3. You must be prepared to defend your bill against arguments given by citizens who do not support it. List the reasons you think opponents of the bill might give for not having the law. Give your response to each reason you list.
   a. Reason: _____
      Response: _____
   b. Reason: _____
      Response: _____

4. If you are not an elected council member, temporarily replace one of the students who is. Now that you have written your bill and prepared for the debate, present it to the class. Give citizens in your class time to debate the bill. List any points in favor of your bill or arguments against it you had not anticipated that are mentioned during the debate.
   a. Points in favor: _____
      _____
   b. Arguments against: _____
      _____

5. Revise the wording of your bill based on comments made during the debate. _____
   _____
   _____

6. Present your revised bill to the class. After completing any further discussion, have the council vote on your bill. What were the results of the vote?
   _____ votes for the bill.
   _____ votes against the bill.

7. Based on this experience, what would you do differently if you were proposing this bill again?
   _____
   _____

LEGAL ADVICE

Activity E
Chapter 27

Name _____

Date _____ Period _____

Invite a lawyer to class or interview one. Find out the answers to the questions below.

1. What are the most common reasons people seek the advice of a lawyer? _____
_____

2. What is the best way to find a lawyer? _____
_____

3. Are there any drawbacks to finding a lawyer through the Yellow Pages? If so, what are they? _____
_____

4. How useful is a state legal association in helping someone find a lawyer? _____
_____

5. In what types of legal services do you specialize? _____
_____

6. How important is it to choose a lawyer who is qualified to deal with a particular type of legal problem? Why is it important? _____
_____

7. On the average, how much do legal services cost? _____

8. Where can someone who is unable to afford a lawyer get legal help? _____

9. How adequate are free legal services provided by a public service agency? _____

10. What problems could arise if a person fails to consult a lawyer in each of the following situations?

    a. When buying a house. _____
    _____

    b. When getting a divorce. _____
    _____

    c. When breaking a lease. _____
    _____

    d. After receiving a summons or subpoena. _____
    _____

    e. After being arrested. _____
    _____

    f. When making out a will. _____
    _____

    g. When settling an estate. _____
    _____

    h. When trying to resolve a consumer problem. _____
    _____

WRITING A COMPLAINT LETTER

Activity F
Chapter 27

Name _____

Date _____ Period _____

Write a complaint letter about one of the following consumer problem situations. Make up any missing details. Be sure to use proper business letter format, as shown on page 331 of the text.
   a. You bought a tube of Brite White toothpaste. The label on the toothpaste claimed that your teeth would be noticeably whiter after using the toothpaste for just one week. You've been using the toothpaste for 10 days and you still haven't noticed a difference.
   b. You bought Old Favorites Jean Softener, a kit designed to give new blue jeans an old, faded look. You followed the directions on the package exactly. When you took your jeans out of the fading solution, they fell apart at the seams.
   c. You bought a Plushy Puppy stuffed toy for your nephew's birthday. When you were wrapping it, one of the eyes fell off. You noticed that the eye had a sharp point on it. You are concerned that your nephew could have been cut if he had been playing with the toy.

28 ENTREPRENEURSHIP

REINFORCING VOCABULARY

Activity A
Chapter 28

Name _____

Date _____ Period _____

Fill in the blanks with the correct chapter terms and find the terms in the word maze. (Terms are located forward, backward, horizontally, vertically, and diagonally in the maze.)

```
E A Q E Y N C O N N I E L A M W
N N Z P I A B C T E D I E P J F
T R T A G I R R E D A I R U R F
R I H R N A Y R T L J D I E N
A S S T E P I S E H M I L K D Z
Q E L N D P T R I C C O R P L L
U C P E X F R A N C H I S E O L
Q I H R T O B E M U S O N O H R
T V T S P W R I N S X T E G K O
C R A H K U T F F E J S V S C B
E E L I N G P V R A U W R X O Y
Y S O P N E U R A Z L R I G T N
E E A U B O V E N U C H S Y S E
J R C O R P O R A T I O N H I H
A V R U D V U F Z W W D E B I C
Y I P I H S R O T E I R P O R P
```

_____ 1. A business that can legally act as a single person, even though many people may own it is called a(n) _____.

_____ 2. A(n) _____ business is one that sells products.

_____ 3. Starting and owning a business of your own is called _____.

_____ 4. The easiest type of business to start and dissolve is a sole _____.

_____ 5. Someone who owns part of a corporation is a(n) _____.

_____ 6. The right to sell a company's products in a specified area is known as a(n) _____.

_____ 7. A(n) _____ is the type of business organization formed when two or more people combine their money and energy.

_____ 8. A(n) _____ business is one in which tasks are performed for customers.

RETAIL AND SERVICE BUSINESSES

Activity B Name _____

Chapter 28 Date _____ Period _____

Answer the following questions about retail and service businesses.

1. What kinds of retail businesses do you patronize? _____
   _____

2. List five retail businesses in your community and identify the types of products sold by each one.

   Business   Products

   a. _____   _____
   b. _____   _____
   c. _____   _____
   d. _____   _____
   e. _____   _____

3. If you were starting a retail business, what kinds of products would you like to sell? _____
   _____

4. Why would you like to sell these kinds of products? _____
   _____

5. Why do you think people would want to buy these kinds of products? _____
   _____

6. List three franchise businesses in your community.

   a. _____
   b. _____
   c. _____

7. If you were starting a business, would you rather start a one-of-a-kind business or a franchise business? Explain your answer. _____
   _____

8. What kinds of service businesses do you patronize? _____
   _____

9. List five service businesses in your community and identify the type of service provided by each one.

   Business   Service

   a. _____   _____
   b. _____   _____
   c. _____   _____
   d. _____   _____
   e. _____   _____

10. If you were starting a service business, what kind of service would you like to provide? _____
    _____

11. Why would you like to provide this kind of service? _____
    _____

12. Why do you think people would be willing to pay for this kind of service? _____
    _____

IS ENTREPRENEURSHIP FOR YOU?

Activity C   Name _____

Chapter 28   Date _____ Period _____

Answer the following questions to help you determine if you might want to become an entrepreneur someday.

1. Which of the following goals do you have for your career? (Check all that apply.)

   _____ To make a lot of money.

   _____ To do your job better than another company or person.

   _____ To develop a new idea.

   _____ To be your own boss.

   _____ To set your own working hours.

   _____ To make your own decisions.

   _____ To gain recognition in the community.

2. Answer the following questions by checking the "Yes" column or the "No" column.

	Yes	No
a. Do you have a good imagination?	_____	_____
b. Do you think you could manage a business successfully?	_____	_____
c. Do you often think of creative ways to solve problems?	_____	_____
d. Do you have lots of ambition and drive?	_____	_____
e. Do you have a good knowledge of a product you would like to sell or a service you would like to provide?	_____	_____
f. Can you make decisions?	_____	_____
g. Can you supervise people fairly well?	_____	_____
h. Can you motivate people to do their work well?	_____	_____
i. Are you comfortable around people you don't know?	_____	_____

3. Which of the following aspects of entrepreneurship would discourage you from starting your own business? (Check all that apply.)

   _____ Long working hours.

   _____ High level of stress.

   _____ Financial risk.

4. What would you consider to be the biggest advantage of owning your own business? Explain your answer.

   _____

   _____

5. What would you consider to be the biggest disadvantage of owning your own business? Explain your answer. _____

   _____

   _____

6. Do you think you would like to be an entrepreneur? Explain why or why not? _____

   _____

   _____

BUSINESS ADVICE

Activity D   Name _____

Chapter 28   Date _____ Period _____

Invite an entrepreneur to class or interview one. Find out the answers to the questions below.

Entrepreneur: _____

Business: _____

1. What kinds of products or services do you offer? _____
   _____

2. How long have you been in business? _____
   _____

3. What type of business organization do you have (sole proprietorship, partnership, or corporation)? Why did you choose that type of organization? _____
   _____

4. When did you first think about becoming an entrepreneur? _____

5. What was your main reason for wanting to start your own business? _____
   _____

6. Give a brief history of your business. _____
   _____
   _____
   _____
   _____

7. If you were starting over today, what would you do differently? _____
   _____

8. If you were starting over today, what would you do the same? _____
   _____

9. What have you found to be the biggest challenge of owning your own business? _____
   _____

10. What have you found to be the greatest reward of owning your own business? _____
    _____

11. What do you feel are the most important characteristics for an entrepreneur to have? _____
    _____

12. What advice would you offer to someone who was thinking about becoming an entrepreneur? ___
    _____
    _____
    _____
    _____

PLANNING A BUSINESS

Activity E   Name _____

Chapter 28   Date _____ Period _____

You don't have to be an adult to be an entrepreneur! Complete this activity to plan a business you could start right now.

1. What type of business do you want to have? _____

2. List any hobbies, classes, part-time jobs, or other experiences you've had that relate to this business.
   _____

3. What will you call your business? _____

4. Who will your customers be? (Consider age, sex, lifestyle, and any other characteristics that you think might affect the willingness of people to use your products or services.) _____
   _____

5. In the chart below, list all of the equipment and supplies you would need to start your business. Be sure to specify how many of each item you would need. For each item listed, check the appropriate column to indicate whether you would borrow it, buy it used, or buy it new. Estimate a cost for each item you would need to buy.

Item	Borrow	Buy Used	Buy New	Estimated Cost
			Total	

6. Can this business be run out of your home? _____

   If not, where will you set up your business? _____
   _____

   How much will this cost? _____

7. How will you advertise your business? _____
   _____

   How much will it cost? _____

8. Can you run this business by yourself? _____

   If not, who will you get to help you? _____
   _____

   How much will this cost? _____

(Continued)

Name _____

9. Use the cost information from items 5 through 8 to estimate your total expenses for one week.
   _____

10. In the first column of the chart below, list a sampling of the products or services you will offer. In the second column, estimate how many of each product you will sell or how many times you will provide each service per week. In the third column, indicate how much you plan to charge for each product or service. Enter your total estimated income from each item in the last column. (Find this by multiplying the second and third columns for each item.)

Product or Service	# per Week	Cost per Item	Total Income per Item
		Total Income per Week	

11. Subtract your estimate of total expenses per week (#9) from your estimate of total income per week (#10).
   _____ − _____ = _____
   Will you make a profit or suffer a loss? _____

12. Would you like to really try putting this plan into action? Explain why or why not. _____
   _____
   _____
   _____
   _____

BUSINESS ORGANIZATIONS

Activity F　　　　　　　　　　　　　Name _____

Chapter 28　　　　　　　　　　　　Date _____ Period _____

Use information from the chapter and library resources to investigate the different types of business organizations. Complete the chart below, listing the advantages and disadvantages of each type of organization. Then answer the question that follows.

TYPE OF ORGANIZATION	ADVANTAGES	DISADVANTAGES
Sole Proprietorship		
Partnership		
Corporation		

If you were starting a business, which type of business organization would you use? Explain your answer.

_____

_____

_____

_____

Planning a Business　143